# Security as Code
*DevSecOps Patterns with AWS*

*BK Sarthak Das and Virginia Chu*

Beijing · Boston · Farnham · Sebastopol · Tokyo

**Security as Code**

by BK Sarthak Das and Virginia Chu

Published by O'Reilly Media, Inc., 1005 Gravenstein Highway North, Sebastopol, CA 95472.

O'Reilly books may be purchased for educational, business, or sales promotional use. Online editions are also available for most titles (*http://oreilly.com*). For more information, contact our corporate/institutional sales department: 800-998-9938 or *corporate@oreilly.com*.

| | |
|---|---|
| **Acquisitions Editors:** Jennifer Pollock, Simina Calin | **Indexer:** Sam Arnold-Boyd |
| **Development Editor:** Sarah Grey | **Interior Designer:** David Futato |
| **Production Editor:** Clare Laylock | **Cover Designer:** Karen Montgomery |
| **Copyeditor:** Nicole Taché | **Illustrator:** Kate Dullea |
| **Proofreader:** Rachel Head | |

January 2023: First Edition

**Revision History for the First Edition**

2023-01-03: First Release

See *http://oreilly.com/catalog/errata.csp?isbn=9781098127466* for release details.

This work is part of a collaboration between O'Reilly and NGINX. See our statement of editorial independence (*https://oreil.ly/editorial-independence*).

978-1-098-12746-6

[LSI]

# Table of Contents

# Preface

The authors of this book work with enterprise AWS customers who have business-critical applications running in the cloud, so we think about security on a daily basis. In recent years, we've noticed that the term *DevSecOps* pops up in nearly every security strategy discussion. Everyone wants it, but not as many people understand it—and it seems like almost nobody knows where to start or what to do.

DevSecOps is a relatively new field, and few books are available to guide those who want to learn more about it. We decided to write this book to help fill that gap by showing you how and where to get started on DevSecOps in AWS.

This book is not an enterprise-grade solution kit for copying and pasting into production (and since every project and organization has different needs, we sincerely hope you would never do that!). Instead, it's designed to introduce you to the building blocks of the DevSecOps mindset, and to guide you along the way with practical examples. We use popular open source tools where possible, to show you that it's not always necessary to buy expensive products to do security the right way.

We use a fictitious company called Automatoonz to illustrate some of the real-world issues you're likely to face in your DevSecOps journey. As we discuss a problem, the Automatoonz team works on it too, giving you a sense of how real teams approach solving the problem at hand. Although the scenarios are fictionalized, these examples come from our extensive personal experience, and we think they'll resonate with you. The solutions we provide in this book are intended as guidance on the art of the possible.

## Who Is This Book For?

This book is for AWS security engineers, DevOps engineers, security analysts, security engineering managers, and other practitioners and leaders at intermediate and senior levels who want to automate more of their security. We recommend that readers have some practical AWS development knowledge and familiarity with Git before starting this book: ideally, enough to do basic coding and debugging within AWS. In Chapter 2, for example, we use CloudFormation, Python, and Kubernetes to demonstrate Infrastructure as Code. You should also be comfortable navigating Git repositories.

## What Do You Need To Get Started?

In practical terms, aside from intermediate knowledge of AWS, to follow the exercises in this book you will need an AWS account where you can deploy. You will also need to install the following, if you do not already have them:

- AWS Command Line Interface (AWS CLI) (latest version)
- Access to an AWS account
- Docker (Community Edition)
- Python (version 3.x.x or higher)
- Git (latest version)
- Kubectl (latest version)
- Kubernetes (version 1.21 or higher)

Chapter 2 has a detailed walkthrough of setting up all these tools.

You will also need access to the book's GitHub repository (*https://oreil.ly/SaCgh*), which includes code samples and other supplemental materials.

## What's in This Book?

We've tried to ensure that the seven chapters in this book are as independent as possible from one another, so that you can pick it up at any point. However, we recommend that you start from the beginning.

Chapter 1 will introduce you to what DevSecOps is, why it is important, and what kind of mindset you'll need to get started. Chapter 2 helps you install the software you'll need for the rest of the book, then walks you through a sample application built with secure configurations to ensure you have your toolkit working. In Chapter 3, you'll learn how to validate Infrastructure as Code to make your resources secure. Chapter 4 looks at how to set up appropriate logging and monitoring to identify and debug issues with your infrastructure.

In Chapter 5, you'll learn about controlling access through automation, including assessing your organization's identity and access management (IAM) policies and refining them according to the principle of least privilege. Chapter 6 is all about testing: we'll introduce you to the practice of Chaos Engineering, show you how to use it to make your infrastructure more resilient, and discuss how to focus on possible points of failure. Finally, in Chapter 7, we wrap up with a look at the roles and processes that should be part of any DevSecOps team.

## Conventions Used in This Book

The following typographical conventions are used in this book:

*Italic*

Indicates new terms, URLs, email addresses, filenames, and file extensions.

`Constant width`

Used for program listings, as well as within paragraphs to refer to program elements such as variable or function names, databases, data types, environment variables, statements, and keywords.

**`Constant width bold`**

Shows commands or other text that should be typed literally by the user.

*`Constant width italic`*

Shows text that should be replaced with user-supplied values or by values determined by context.

 This element signifies a tip or suggestion.

 This element signifies a general note.

 This element indicates a warning or caution.

## Using Code Examples

Code examples are available for download at *https://oreil.ly/SaCgh*.

If you have a technical question or a problem using the code examples, please send email to *bookquestions@oreilly.com*.

This book is here to help you get your job done. In general, if example code is offered with this book, you may use it in your programs and documentation. You do not need to contact us for permission unless you're reproducing a significant portion of the code. For example, writing a program that uses several chunks of code from this book does not require permission. Selling or distributing examples from O'Reilly books does require permission. Answering a question by citing this book and quoting example code does not require permission. Incorporating a significant amount of example code from this book into your product's documentation does require permission.

We appreciate, but generally do not require, attribution. An attribution usually includes the title, author, publisher, and ISBN. For example: "*Security as Code: DevSecOps Patterns with AWS* by BK Sarthak Das and Virginia Chu (O'Reilly). Copyright 2023 Virginia Chu and BK Sarthak Das, 978-1-098-12746-6."

If you feel your use of code examples falls outside fair use or the permission given above, feel free to contact us at *permissions@oreilly.com*.

# O'Reilly Online Learning

O'REILLY® For more than 40 years, *O'Reilly Media* has provided technology and business training, knowledge, and insight to help companies succeed.

Our unique network of experts and innovators share their knowledge and expertise through books, articles, and our online learning platform. O'Reilly's online learning platform gives you on-demand access to live training courses, in-depth learning paths, interactive coding environments, and a vast collection of text and video from O'Reilly and 200+ other publishers. For more information, visit *https://oreilly.com*.

# How to Contact Us

Please address comments and questions concerning this book to the publisher:

O'Reilly Media, Inc.
1005 Gravenstein Highway North
Sebastopol, CA 95472
800-998-9938 (in the United States or Canada)
707-829-0515 (international or local)
707-829-0104 (fax)

We have a web page for this book, where we list errata, examples, and any additional information. You can access this page at *https://oreil.ly/SecurityAsCode*.

Email *bookquestions@oreilly.com* to comment or ask technical questions about this book.

For news and information about our books and courses, visit *https://oreilly.com*.

Find us on LinkedIn: *https://linkedin.com/company/oreilly-media*.

Follow us on Twitter: *https://twitter.com/oreillymedia*.

Watch us on YouTube: *https://youtube.com/oreillymedia*.

# Acknowledgments

There are numerous people who are responsible for this book.

We would like to take the time to thank our amazing and wonderful team at O'Reilly Media (Sarah Grey, development editor; Nicole Taché, freelance editor; and Clare Laylock, production editor) for their professionalism, commitment, and guidance in publishing a book. We learned that writing a book is not easy or trivial.

Our grateful and humble thanks go to our technical reviewer Joe Milligan. It has been an honor to collaborate with him.

BK would like to thank his close friends and family for being supportive throughout the process of writing this book.

Virginia would like to thank her family, four-legged sounding board, and close friends for their support and patience throughout this adventure. Special thanks to her mentor Michael Hausenblas for inspiring her to work on this book.

Finally, we would like to thank all the wonderful contributors and developers for the tools we have used in our book.

# CHAPTER 1

# Introduction to DevSecOps

We did not start our careers in security, but we both know that delivering software is of utmost importance to developers. "Delivering software" in this context means delivering *something that does what it is supposed to do*. This could refer to the code being stable, or the software meeting the functional requirements (for example, a calculator can add, multiply, subtract, and divide numbers) and performance expectations without any issues (for example, a chat application allows more than 10 people to send messages to each other simultaneously).

Building *quality* software, however, requires good coding practices, resilient architectures, and security. It's common for security to be added into the software after it has been built, but the *shift-left* approach (*https://oreil.ly/IEkGF*) recommends moving security to much earlier in the development life cycle, building it in from the start. We will discuss that approach in this chapter, focusing on *Security as Code* (SaC). In this approach, our infrastructure's security policies—detection, prevention, remediation— are all defined as code.

We will also discuss DevSecOps in this chapter, focusing on the three major players in software development:

*Development*
Is your code doing what it is meant to do?

*Operations*
What is this code running on? Do you have the required skills/time to maintain this going forward? Can the provisioned infrastructure handle the expected workload?

*Testing*
Can the code survive unexpected use cases? How does the code respond to something you didn't account for?

The primary focus of this book is how to integrate security into your development process through cloud infrastructure. Declaring infrastructure in files is also known as *Infrastructure as Code* (IaC). Kief Morris provides a helpful definition in his book *Infrastructure as Code*, 2nd edition (O'Reilly):

> Infrastructure as Code is an approach to infrastructure automation based on practices from software development. It emphasizes consistent, repeatable routines for provisioning and changing systems and their configuration. You make changes to code, then use automation to test and apply those changes to your systems.

Using IaC and declaring the security aspects of that infrastructure is Security as Code (SaC). SaC is not entirely different from IaC, but rather focuses on enabling security controls using templates.

This chapter introduces the basic concepts of SaC, and Chapter 2 provides setup and instructions to get you started. After that, the chapters are organized by security domains. Some chapters are exclusive to a single domain; others address multiple domains in a single stage of the buildout. Each domain has its own unique set of questions. For instance:

*Data protection (Chapter 3)*
    Is everything encrypted? Does the encryption approach follow data classification policies? Do we have data classification implemented?

*Infrastructure security (Chapter 3)*
    As we are running our application in the cloud, is all the infrastructure deployed securely? Is our S3 bucket publicly accessible when it should not be? Can we prevent deployment of our resources when something is missing?

*Application security (Chapter 3)*
    Is the code we're running secure? How many active vulnerabilities are there in our code? Did we release code with a critical vulnerability?

*Logging and monitoring (Chapter 4)*
    Do we know what to monitor? When does an observation become an anomaly? Are the right application security indicators in place to inform us of any mishap?

*Identity and access management (Chapter 5)*
    Who has access to what? Does anyone have any elevated privileges? Can someone elevate their own or others' privileges?

*Incident response (Chapter 6)*
    How do we react to incidents? Can we replace part of the offending application when something goes wrong?

Throughout the chapters, we will use Amazon Web Services (AWS) native security services and best practices to baseline the environment we are deploying. When we assume certain operational and team structures, we explicitly call out those assumptions.

# Before DevOps: The Software Development Life Cycle

When you are new in your career, writing a piece of code that does exactly what was asked is a joy of its own. With time, however, we've realized writing quality code does not stop at making 2 + 2 = 4. What if the user enters "2 + a"? How should your software behave?

Well, that's the responsibility of the Quality and Testing engineers, isn't it? Wrong.

We've seen back-and-forth between developers and testers that was time-consuming and created unhealthy expectations from both teams. Let's take the example of the calculator input of "2 + a". If, as a coder, you did not think of this use case because it was not part of the requirements, and your tester or QA team did not record it as a test case, you would be shipping broken code to your customers. This broken code would be your final product. A codebase that doesn't work as expected is not a joy for the end user to work with.

Code needs to be hosted on some infrastructure to be built and deployed. Is it going to run on a server in your datacenter, on a virtual machine in the cloud, on a container, or on someone's laptop? Depending on your answer, you have another set of responsibilities related to infrastructure. Once you set up your infrastructure, you will need to answer a new series of questions, including:

- Are the coders developing this on the exact same platform on which it will be deployed?
- Who is setting up all the infrastructure?
- Does the infrastructure fail open or fail safe, in the case of an error?

That set of questions needs another set of tests to make sure that the application code is being run correctly on the right platform, and that the platform is not misbehaving.

In traditional software development, only *developers* take care of development, which means their prime directive is writing code to a specification. The *operations* team handles the environment and method of deployment, and the change management procedures. *Testers* take the output of the developers and the operations team and make sure the near-final product does not break. These three roles are not mutually exclusive, but each team needs to wait for input from the previous team to start its work.

A very common representation of this flow is the Software Development Life Cycle (SDLC) model (see Figure 1-1). In practice, the waterfall model of the SDLC might operate something like this: developers create code quickly, based on functional requirements. The code is sent for testing, errors are found, and the code is sent back to developers. The developers fix the code and send it for another round of testing. Once the testing is complete, the code is handed off to the operations team for maintenance.

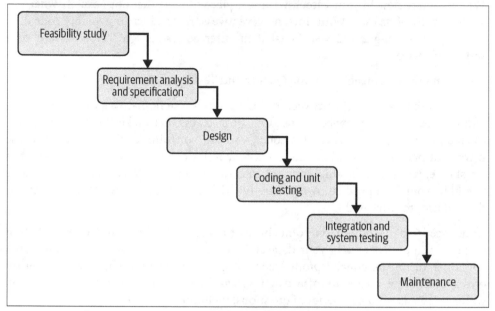

*Figure 1-1. Software Development Life Cycle: waterfall model (https://oreil.ly/KtVv0)*

Siloed teams operating in a hands-off style, similar to the SDLC in Figure 1-1, have their disadvantages. Each team has its own toolset and handles a very specific piece of the SDLC, and is typically unaware of the toolsets of the other teams. This makes it difficult to get quality software out the door on time.

The waterfall model leads to a lot of back-and-forth between teams, as we've noted. The back-and-forth is made worse when you have not delivered anything because your code has not passed your testing teams. So, a whole lot of time and effort is lost without producing any tangible outcomes.

Enter DevOps. In order to reduce time to market and improve the quality of software, the concept of DevOps was introduced. In their book *Effective DevOps* (O'Reilly), authors Jennifer Davis and Ryn Daniels define DevOps as:

A cultural movement that changes how individuals think about their work, values the diversity of work done, supports intentional processes that accelerate the rate by which businesses realize value, and measures the effect of social and technical change. It is a way of thinking and a way of working that enables individuals and organizations to develop and maintain sustainable work practices. It is a cultural framework for sharing stories and developing empathy, enabling people and teams to practice their crafts in effective and lasting ways.

In a DevOps model, the development, testing, and operations teams don't work in silos, but are the same group. If we were to visualize the DevOps model, it would look like a homogeneous blob of roles. Kief Morris writes in *Infrastructure as Code* that the goal of DevOps is:

> To reduce barriers and friction between organizational silos—development, operations, and other stakeholders involved in planning, building, and running software. Although technology is the most visible, and in some ways simplest face of DevOps, it's culture, people, and processes that have the most impact on flow and effectiveness. Technology and engineering practices like Infrastructure as Code should be used to support efforts to bridge gaps and improve collaboration.

We want to emphasize this point: *DevOps is not solely enabled by technology. It is effective only when people, processes, and technology are working together.* There is a common misconception that if you use tools that are used in CI/CD systems, you're automatically practicing DevOps. This is flawed thinking. What enables DevOps is collaboration.

---

### Recommendations for Further Reading

The basics of DevOps, modern architectures, and application security are all outside the scope of this book, but we recommend the following references if you want to learn more:

*DevOps*
- *Effective DevOps* by Jennifer Davis and Ryn Daniels (O'Reilly)
- *Understanding Agile DevOps* by Jim Bird (O'Reilly)
- *DevOps Tools for Java Developers* by Stephen Chin, Melissa McKay, Ixchel Ruiz, and Baruch Sadogursky (O'Reilly)

*Modern architectures*
- *Building Microservices*, 2nd edition, by Sam Newman (O'Reilly)
- *Building Event-Driven Microservices* by Adam Bellemare (O'Reilly)
- *Fundamentals of Software Architecture* by Mark Richards and Neal Ford (O'Reilly)

---

*Application security*
- *Shifting Left for Application Security* by Peter Conrad (O'Reilly)
- *Agile Application Security* by Laura Bell, Michael Brunton-Spall, Rich Smith, and Jim Bird (O'Reilly)

# What Is DevSecOps?

DevSecOps is not a "new version" of DevOps, but rather a conscious effort to add security into your DevOps framework. Like with DevOps, there are numerous definitions of and approaches to DevSecOps. For the purposes of this book, we define *DevSecOps* as the ability to implement and deploy SaC in software.

We will be leaning heavily on APIs, cloud services, and other open source projects to implement SaC. When a part of your SDLC becomes "as code," your team should have the openness to build things.

As your organization begins to implement DevSecOps, there are two important things your team will need to outline: tools and security guidelines.

First, how will you write your IaC? In other words, what tools will you use? This could be a tool like AWS CloudFormation or Terraform. There are numerous services and products available from vendors and the open source community that you can use to build and integrate SaC into your pipeline. As we mentioned, this book will use AWS and open source projects to demonstrate the *why* and *how* of doing DevSecOps, instead of fixating on a particular tool's licensing or procurement. We chose to focus on AWS in this book since it is currently the most popular cloud infrastructure vendor, controlling 33% of the market (*https://oreil.ly/mlGjk*). However, the book's underlying principles will be useful to all readers.

Second, what are your company's security "rules of the road"? What has your security team designated as "definitely don't do this" rules? Understanding why the security team provides certain guidance helps you understand the concerns underlying the rules.

In DevSecOps, you are building security directly into your software development pipeline (see Figure 1-2). In step 1, the developer lints their code locally and makes sure its formatting follows the team's conventions and standards. They then commit the code to the repository. In step 2, the build system of the pipeline scans for errors and any other vulnerabilities and misconfigurations. The security of the pipeline is built into this stage. Finally, in step 3, the code is (possibly) ready for deployment. The last hurdle is a *decision gate*—a mechanism that checks for errors. If any errors are found, deployment is canceled and the developer is informed. If the code has no errors, the deployment goes through.

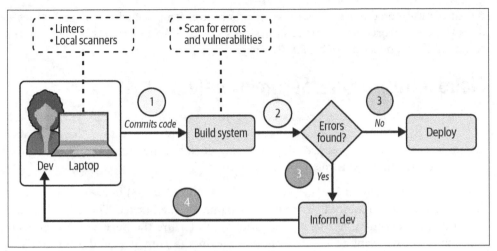

*Figure 1-2. Building security into a DevOps pipeline*

Steps 1 and 2 happen every time. The top version of step 3 only occurs when the linters and scanners discover no errors. Both the lower version of step 3 and step 4 only occur when the linters and scanners discover an issue.

The code that is deployed is not the only thing that needs to be secured. You also need to protect the security checks you are implementing within the DevOps pipeline. Imagine for a moment that anyone who commits code can turn security checks on and off. Would it be secure?

We have seen teams bypass their security checks because an "urgent" code change was needed and it was faster to deploy without security. That is a recipe for disaster. Situations where a real emergency justifies a nonsecured code change should be recorded and remediated. There should not be a bypass function for deployments.

# Introducing Automatoonz

Security is a broad topic. Its subfields include physical security, application security, cryptography, training, and many more. We will limit our scope in this book to a subset of security domains, which we'll explore by following the journey of an imaginary company we'll call Automatoonz.

Automatoonz is an animation company that's recently been getting into web toons and series creation. The company operates on AWS and is currently trying to build security into its development and deployment processes. It wants to be lean and secure, but the company is relatively new in the space and doesn't have the funding to hire more security engineers. Thus, its aim is to automate as much security as possible.

Because Automatoonz operates on AWS, there are some security responsibilities it doesn't have to worry about, such as physical security. AWS refers to this as the shared responsibility model (*https://oreil.ly/Hc1vk*).

# Cloud Infrastructure: Secure by Default

In cloud infrastructure, every resource is created through an API call. Each API call has parameters that configure your resource exactly as you want it. The software development kit (SDK) you use will also automatically generate a default configuration, to provide maximum customization options.

For example, if you are using the AWS SDK for Python (Boto3) to create an Amazon S3 bucket, the only required parameter is a name for the bucket. The SDK does not ask you for encryption, nor does it require you to ensure the bucket is not publicly accessible. If you want to enforce encryption on the contents of the bucket, you should do so upon deployment. This is what is referred to as *Secure by Default*.

Secure by Default does not mean you should lock down everything you possibly can. It's often said that the safest computer system is the one that's unplugged. But, if you make your system so secure that it's practically unusable—well, people won't use it. They'll look for workarounds, potentially compromising security in the process. In this book, we aim to demonstrate *usable security*—a balance between usability and security.

In an IaC paradigm, you can *templatize* your resources—make declarative code for patterns you come across and create templates that developers can work from, in order to keep the codebase consistent. For example, if you are building a web server within AWS, you should be able to standardize the architecture for future deployments. If the architecture is defined only in a diagram, you'll need to codify that diagram as IaC. To do so, you'll need to create declarative templates so that the same web server pattern can be deployed repeatedly with zero deviation.

What does templatization provide in terms of security? Let's revisit the S3 bucket example. At Automatoonz, the legal team is tasked with ensuring that all of the company's data is *encrypted at rest*, meaning that data stored in any persistent storage has to be encrypted through a cryptographic key, which is only accessible to authorized users. In cloud computing, you can define encryption at rest through API flags in your IaC templates. This also helps standardize a Secure by Default posture for your infrastructure.

Of course, the legal team informs the developers of this requirement, and the developers need to apply the right checks and balances to adhere to the policy. If there is an IaC template for the bucket, the developers must check it before it is sent to AWS endpoints for resource creation. This will prevent the unencrypted bucket from ever being created.

At a very high level, Figure 1-3 shows what we are trying to achieve. The developer on the left creates an AWS CloudFormation template, which in turn creates an S3 bucket. This goes to a decision gate. If encryption is not enabled, the decision gate shuts down deployment. Only after the template is fixed can the deployment go through.

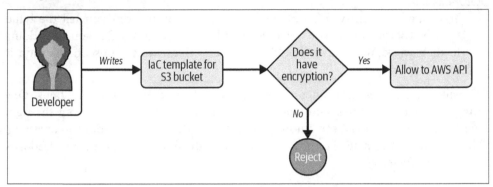

*Figure 1-3. Decision gate that rejects unencrypted S3 bucket templates*

# Move Fast, Secure Fast: The Importance of Automation

When you drive a car, there are certain rules of the road that you must obey. Not adhering to these rules can lead to mishaps, serious accidents, and legal trouble. In security, we have similar invariable rules. Sometimes the rules are driven by regulatory or compliance requirements; other times they're intended to create engineering excellence. Regardless of the reason, every team is expected to follow these rules.

How can developers ensure they consistently follow rules related to security? Recall our earlier discussion of IaC, and its ability to define cloud resources in a declarative manner. Herein lies our answer. If we can set predictable flags and/or parameters for cloud resources, we can allow operations such as creating new resources or deploying new code to go through *only* if certain things are present.

When you want to move at the speed of the cloud, you want to secure things at the speed of the cloud as well. This means automating as much of your security as possible. There is a manual way of doing the check shown in Figure 1-3, in which the developer looks at their code and prevents a misconfiguration. But remember the old adage, "Humans are the weakest link in security"? You ideally want to automate these checks. To automate a security check—a central idea in DevSecOps—there are certain attributes to consider:

*Idempotence*
    The security check should yield the same results no matter how many times you pass the template in question.

*Baseline*

> The security check should apply to all or most resources. If a security check only applies to one variant of a resource, which appears in less than 30% of your deployments, you will get a lot of noise and failures while doing the check.

*Recommendation*

> You found a security misconfiguration. That's cool, but did you tell the build system what to do? If you leave your end users without a fix, you are adding to their work. Your scans should recommend fixes when a misconfiguration is found.

We will be using these attributes as we build our pipeline throughout the book. One thing we want to reiterate: automation does *not* solve everything. Without the right owners and processes, all the automation in the world will not amount to anything. These security checks need to be maintained, and the developer should give feedback to improve efficiency.

# DevSecOps Culture

Technology is not a silver bullet. Culture plays a role, too. DevOps at its core is built on a culture, and its tools are only useful when people use them in the right ways.

We have seen organizations acquire every possible tool that claims to solve security issues, yet not even configure half of them. Why aren't the teams using these security tools? Do they lack training? Are the tools overkill, or too expensive to roll out to the entire organization?

We highly recommend answering one simple question before you buy any security tool: *What security problem are you trying to solve?* Answers like "make things secure" and "improve my security" are as vague as it gets. Try to boil it down to a single sentence. If that doesn't give you a clear answer, consider writing a risk statement. A risk statement looks something like this:

> Lack of X leads to loss of Y because of Z.
>
> X = a security function, like access control or logging
> Y = the impact if your security control is not implemented (i.e., what is at stake?)
> Z = how your security control prevents a security event

We won't go into detail on procurement, but it is crucial to understand what security problem a tool is meant to solve before buying it. A lot of enterprise-grade tools offer free trials or demos. If your team has a builder mindset, you may want to explore the vast expanse of open source cloud security tools, many of which have made their mark in the industry and continue to get better.

---

Once you've selected a tool, who will maintain it? Will it need to be updated regularly? Your tool should have a clear owner on the operational side. Let's say you get a cloud security posture management (CSPM) tool, and the security team has integrated every cloud account to be ingested. The security team receives alerts from the accounts, but takes no action because it expects the cloud account owner to act on those alerts. But the cloud account owner thinks the security team is handling it. Without a clear process for addressing the alerts, the teams have no plan of action. Simple tools like responsibility assignment matrices (or RACI charts) and runbooks can take care of this. We discuss these tools in more detail in Chapter 7.

# Summary

Now that we have introduced DevSecOps and clarified the scope of the book, let's start implementing DevSecOps into our pipeline!

The subsequent chapters will begin by setting up the infrastructure for Automatoonz and iteratively building security capabilities into the application development process. We will primarily focus on the technology and tooling, but we will call out any people and process must-haves, derived from our experience.

A quick recap of key takeaways from this chapter:

- DevSecOps is a variant of DevOps that includes security in its iterative DevOps model.
- If you can prevent misconfigured resources from being created, you can create security hygiene and educate developers.
- Automating security checks requires idempotence, baselines, and recommendations. Chapters 3 and 4 address this topic in more detail.
- Automating security checks alone will not solve security problems. Establish people and processes to own and operate the automation.
- Establish *why* you're implementing a security tool before rolling it out.

# Setting Up Your Environment

Now that you're excited and engaged, you're ready to experiment and create something in your AWS account. We'll use free, publicly accessible sample code to demonstrate how you can create or destroy objects or resources with the "magic" of automation.

In this chapter, we'll show you how to set up your local environment with some simple commands. As we discussed in Chapter 1, AWS will be the cloud provider of choice for our Automatoonz adventure in this book.

When you are finished running through the chapter, you will have a fully automated Amazon Elastic Kubernetes Service (EKS) cluster and an AWS Lambda container image pipeline on which to deploy a simple Python application.

 Remember to set up and test your account credentials, and test your access. Also, don't forget to destroy the sample resources you created in your account to avoid inadvertent billing.

## What You'll Need

Here is a list of tools you'll need to follow along with the exercises and activities in this book:

*AWS CLI*
> An open source tool that enables you to interact with AWS services in the assigned account by using commands in your terminal. For more information, visit the official site (*https://oreil.ly/aP1fn*). Please use the latest version.

*AWS CloudFormation*

A service that helps you provision and configure your AWS resources based on a template file written in JSON or YAML. The files are used to deploy and provision infrastructure resources tracked as code. For more information, visit the official site (*https://oreil.ly/qrpCz*).

*Docker (Community Edition)*

A software platform, or platform as a service (PaaS), that bundles software into units called containers. These containers allow you to build, test, and deploy applications. For more information, visit the official site (*https://oreil.ly/jRZzd*). Please use the latest version.

*Python*

An open source, interpreted, object-oriented, high-level programming language with dynamic semantics. For more information, visit the official site (*https://oreil.ly/DzMyD*). Please use version 3.x.x or higher.

*Git*

An open source, distributed version control system for different file types. For more information, visit the official site (*https://oreil.ly/uhWe2*). Please use the latest version.

*Kubernetes*

An open source system for automating deployment, scaling, and management of containerized applications. For more information, visit the official site (*https://oreil.ly/KAaff*). Please use version 1.21 or higher.

*Kubectl*

An open source Kubernetes command-line tool that allows users to interact with Kubernetes clusters. For more information, visit the official site (*https://oreil.ly/gJMfe*). Please use the latest version.

# Installing and Verifying Your Setup

You can use package managers to download the latest versions of tools, or `curl` to directly download the installation packages. Then, extract the installer file and run the install script. This section provides commands for the Darwin, Linux, and Windows operating systems.

## Installing the AWS CLI

Run the appropriate commands to install the AWS CLI, which allows you to interact with your AWS account and manage IaC. (See the official AWS documentation (*https://oreil.ly/HVXUm*) for more details.)

Darwin:

```
> brew install awscli
```

Linux:

```
> curl "https://awscli.amazonaws.com/awscli-exe-linux-<CPU_architecture>.zip"
    -o "awscliv2.zip"

> unzip awscliv2.zip

> sudo ./aws/install
```

Windows:

```
> choco install awscli
```

After the installation, complete the configuration to associate your AWS account (see the documentation (*https://oreil.ly/tfCgE*)). This lets you run the sample code provided in the GitHub repository (*https://oreil.ly/SaCgh*) that accompanies this book.

## Installing the Docker Engine

Run the appropriate commands to install the Docker engine (*https://oreil.ly/MGLSm*). The Docker CLI allows you to interact with your Dockerfile.

Darwin:

```
> brew install docker
```

Linux:

```
> curl -fsSL https://get.docker.com -o get-docker.sh

> sudo sh get-docker.sh
```

Windows:

```
> choco install docker-engine
```

After the installation is complete, test for a response from the Docker CLI.

## Checking Your Python Version

Run the appropriate commands to check if Python version 3.x.x or higher has been installed. Python will be used in the AWS Lambda container in the sample code.

Darwin:

```
> python3 --version
```

Linux:

```
> python3 --version
```

Windows:

```
> python --version
```

If Python 3.x.x is not installed, visit the official site (*https://oreil.ly/QUYlv*) for more information.

## Installing Git

Run the appropriate commands to install Git, the distributed version control system. The Git CLI allows you to interact with Git repositories.

Darwin:

```
> brew install git
```

Linux:

```
> sudo yum install git -y
```

Windows:

```
> choco install git
```

After installation, complete the configuration to associate your personal settings. Then, run a command to test for a response from the Git CLI. For more information or troubleshooting, visit the official site (*https://oreil.ly/YMGrV*).

## Installing Kubernetes

Run the appropriate commands to install the Kubernetes CLI, which will allow you to interact with Git repositories.

Darwin:

```
> brew install kubectl
```

Linux:

```
> curl -LO https://dl.k8s.io/release/$(curl -L -s
    https://dl.k8s.io/release/stable.txt)/bin/linux/amd64/kubectl
```

```
> sudo install -o root -g root -m 0755 kubectl /usr/local/bin/kubectl
```

Windows:

```
> choco install kubernetes-cli
```

After the installation is complete, test for a response from the Kubernetes CLI. For more information or troubleshooting, visit the official site (*https://oreil.ly/EmJTH*).

Now that you've installed and verified your tools, it's time to create a pipeline.

# Creating Your First Bare-Bones Pipeline

Begin creating your pipeline by downloading the latest version of the sample code:

```
> git clone https://github.com/bksarthak/devsecops-book
```

This command will create an AWS Service Catalog portfolio to hold all the AWS Service Catalog infrastructure and cluster products:

```
> aws cloudformation create-stack \
    --template-body file://template/ServiceCatalogPortfolio.yml \
    --stack-name EKSPortfolio \
    --parameters file://parameter/ServiceCatalog.json \
    --capabilities CAPABILITY_NAMED_IAM \
    --region <INPUT_YOUR_REGION>
```

Next, upload all the AWS Service Catalog files and the AWS Lambda function code:

```
> aws s3 cp service_catalog_products/ \
    s3://<s3_bucket_for_sc_products_lambda_function>/ \
    --recursive \
    --exclude "*" \
    --include "*.yml" \
    --include "*.zip" \
    --region <INPUT_YOUR_REGION>
```

Then, add the AWS Service Catalog networking product:

```
> aws cloudformation create-stack \
    --template-body file://template/ServiceCatalogProduct.yml \
    --stack-name EKSNetwork \
    --parameters file://parameter/NetworkProduct.json \
    --region <INPUT_YOUR_REGION>
```

The following command will add the AWS identity and access management (IAM) product role resource, which integrates with the AWS Service Catalog:

```
> aws cloudformation create-stack \
    --template-body file://template/ServiceCatalogProduct.yml \
    --stack-name EKSIAM \
    --parameters file://parameter/IAMProduct.json \
    --region <INPUT_YOUR_REGION>
```

Next, add the AWS Service Catalog EKS Cluster product:

```
> aws cloudformation create-stack \
    --template-body file://template/ServiceCatalogProduct.yml \
    --stack-name EKSCluster \
    --parameters file://parameter/EKSProduct.json \
    --region <INPUT_YOUR_REGION>
```

Add the AWS Service Catalog EKS Nodegroup product:

```
> aws cloudformation create-stack \
    --template-body file://template/eks_nodegroup.yml \
    --stack-name EKSNodegroup \
    --parameters file://parameter/EKSNodeGroupProduct.json \
    --region <INPUT_YOUR_REGION>
```

Add the AWS Service Catalog EKS Lambda product:

```
> aws cloudformation create-stack \
    --template-body file://template/ServiceCatalogProduct.yml \
    --stack-name EKSLambda \
    --parameters file://parameter/EKSLambdaProduct.json \
    --region <INPUT_YOUR_REGION>
```

Add the AWS Service Catalog EKS Virtual Private Cloud (VPC) endpoint product:

```
> aws cloudformation create-stack \
    --template-body file://template/ServiceCatalogProduct.yml \
    --stack-name EKSVPCendpoint \
    --parameters file://parameter/VPCEndpointProduct.json \
    --region <INPUT_YOUR_REGION>
```

And add the AWS Service Catalog EKS control plane logging product:

```
> aws cloudformation create-stack \
    --template-body file://template/ServiceCatalogProduct.yml \
    --stack-name EKSLog \
    --parameters file://parameter/EKSLoggingProduct.json \
    --region <INPUT_YOUR_REGION>
```

If you want to run the steps to create an AWS Service Catalog portfolio and products, run these two bash scripts as a shortcut:

```
> chapter-2/scripts/eks-sc-portfolio.sh # create portfolio
```

```
> chapter-2/scripts/eks-sc-products.sh  # create Service Catalog products
```

Now provision the AWS Service Catalog all products resource into your AWS account:

Note: Please update any placeholder fields in all shell scripts.

```
Key=S3BucketPath,Value=<s3_bucket_for_sc_products_lambda_function>
PROFILE=<INPUT_YOUR_AWS_PROFILE>
REGION=<INPUT_YOUR_REGION>
```

Run this command to deploy your resources:

```
> chapter-2/scripts/eks-provision.sh
```

# Summary

Figure 2-1 diagrams the environment you are deploying in your AWS account.

---

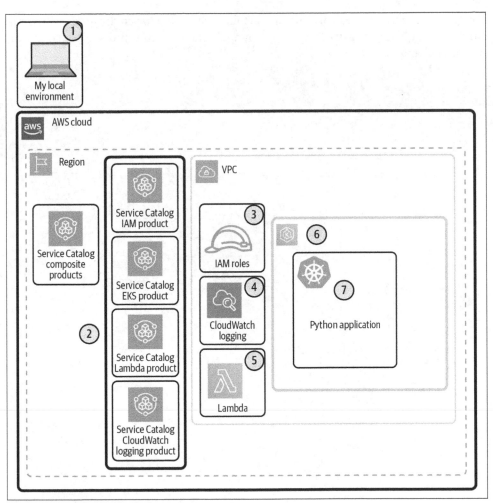

*Figure 2-1. Infrastructure as Code pipeline*

Let's look at the pieces of this pipeline, corresponding to the numbers in Figure 2-1:

1. Your laptop or terminal to upload and download code
2. AWS Service Catalog (manages logical products and modularized code)
3. AWS IAM role to allow access to the EKS cluster
4. Amazon CloudWatch, for logging and metrics
5. AWS Lambda container images and Amazon ECR
6. EKS managed cluster
7. Python application deployed in the EKS cluster

Take a few minutes to look around and get familiar with your environment. Now that you've set up your infrastructure, you can apply the concepts and sample code from the later chapters.

# CHAPTER 3

# Securing Your Infrastructure

As we saw in Chapter 2, cloud infrastructure can be spun up and down considerably faster than traditional datacenter infrastructure. Cloud providers use declarative languages to help end users configure the infrastructure they spin up. For example, AWS uses CloudFormation templates.

In this book, for the sake of simplicity, we'll be using CloudFormation code. However, you should know that there are other IaC tools—such as Cloud Development Kit (CDK) and Hashicorp's Terraform—that use different writing and deployment formats, but achieve the same goal of creating infrastructure through code.

## What Makes Infrastructure Secure?

What does it mean to "secure" your infrastructure? IaC is code, and just like you secure your application's code, you need to plan to secure your IaC. The top three priorities involved in securing IaC are, in order of importance:

1. Preventing unwanted access to your code

2. Detecting misconfigurations in the infrastructure to be deployed

3. Preventing misconfigured code from being deployed

In this chapter, we'll explore all three priorities in detail.

We are assuming that you have an intermediate understanding of how to use Git-based version control and will not be covering Git troubleshooting or branching strategy. For more on those topics, we recommend reading *Head First Git* by Raju Gandhi (O'Reilly) or the Git documentation (*https://oreil.ly/qgpjg*).

We also delve into topics like identity and access management (IAM). We recommend reading the AWS documentation (*https://oreil.ly/jC2FB*) to understand IAM, if you are not familiar with it.

# Hands Off! Preventing Unwanted Access with IAM Permissions

Always store your IaC files in a remote, versioned repository as you integrate changes. AWS has its own native Git-based version control system, known as Code-Commit, which we'll be using throughout this book. Now, how do you secure this repository from unwanted access?

*Identity and access management* (IAM) is the core method of assigning permissions to resources in AWS accounts. Anyone who needs to create, update, or delete files within your CodeCommit repository should—at the bare minimum—have the permissions laid out in the IAM policy. This policy allows CodeCommit actions to be taken in your specific repository only if it is in the correct region: in the following example, for instance, only end users in the us-east-2 region can perform these actions.

The second of the following two statements allows you to list all CodeCommit repositories within your AWS account. We have separated the two statements because you cannot use `ListRepositories` for a specific resource:

```json
{
    "Version": "2012-10-17",
    "Statement": [
        {
            "Effect": "Allow",
            "Action": "codecommit:*",
            "Resource": "arn:aws:codecommit:us-east-2:111111111111:*",
            "Condition": {
                "StringEquals": {
                    "aws:RequestedRegion": "us-east-2"
                }
            }
        },
        {
            "Effect": "Allow",
            "Action": "codecommit:ListRepositories",
            "Resource": "*",
            "Condition": {
```

```
                    "StringEquals": {
                        "aws:RequestedRegion": "us-east-2"
                    }
                }
            }
        ]
    }
```

This IAM policy is a starting point for working with CodeCommit repositories. You can optionally pare these permissions down if you want to limit a user's actions to a specific repository. You can see an example in the book's supplemental materials (*https://oreil.ly/j9gUp*) on GitHub.

# Detecting Misconfigurations

The next step in securing your IaC is to detect any misconfigurations written into it. To explain more about misconfigurations, let's shift our focus back to our fictional company, Automatoonz.

Automatoonz is working to become a fast-moving, developer-focused organization in which security is baked into the development life cycle. Since security has often been treated as an afterthought within their organization, prioritizing it will help front-load initial security patterns and work, allowing the development team to scale with less friction in the future.

The developers are planning to use Amazon EC2 instances (*https://oreil.ly/9Zqig*) to deploy and host an application to be used by customers. Lupe, from the Automatoonz security team, asks the developer team to make sure the volumes attached to the EC2 instances are encrypted. However, Jake, a newly hired DevSecOps engineer, accidentally forgets to encrypt one of the volumes. This mistake is identified during an internal audit, and the developer team rushes to fix it.

Afterward, the developer and security teams want to make sure this mistake never happens again. Rather than depending on human consistency, the teams agree to use automation to find errors in the IaC. They need to decide on some "rules of the road" to ensure that their automations meet compliance standards and pass audits.

## Identifying a Standard

Both teams want to find a baseline standard to secure the IaC—ideally one they can implement quickly. After some research, they find the Center for Internet Security (CIS) (*https://oreil.ly/L6r3f*), a cloud provider–agnostic consortium that provides baseline configurations for different scenarios through its CIS Benchmarks (*https://oreil.ly/cGmZN*) resource. CIS's configurations are considered the industry standard and are updated regularly. The Automatoonz teams decide to use CIS Benchmarks and note that they'll need to track updates to keep up with any changes. Now they need to decide which level of hardening they want as the baseline for their environment.

## Threat Modeling

The CIS Benchmarks are a good starting point, but they don't account for all security considerations. In order to create a custom security action plan, Lupe suggests developing a threat model of the application.

*Threat modeling* is a design tool that helps teams enumerate the possible vulnerabilities in any given application. There are many ways to build a threat model. One of the more popular frameworks is STRIDE (*https://oreil.ly/N0nJJ*), a threat modeling tool that helps identify security risks early in the development cycle. STRIDE includes six categories of security risks, shown in Table 3-1.

*Table 3-1. STRIDE's security risk categories*

| STRIDE category | Definition | What does it mean for Automatoonz? |
| --- | --- | --- |
| Spoofing | Pretending to be someone you are not by using someone else's credentials | Ability to assume the role of CodePipeline to deploy the CloudFormation stack without checks |
| Tampering | Unauthorized changes made to the system (either infrastructure or application) | Direct changes to the application and infrastructure are made without going through the CodePipeline |
| Repudiation | Users denying that they have made changes without other users being able to disprove them | Any changes to the infrastructure cannot be traced back to a log entry |
| Information disclosure | Exposure of information to users who should not have access to the information | Permissions granted to the end users provide visibility into the underlying infrastructure and logs |
| Denial of service | Valid users are not allowed to carry out tasks | Developers are not able to commit their code to CodeCommit |
| Elevation of privilege | Unprivileged user gains access to privileged operations | Users can deploy and spin up resources without going through the CodePipeline checks |

While Table 3-1 is not an exhaustive list of possible threats, they are the ones we'll worry about for our purposes in this chapter. In the next section, we'll focus on various security controls that can protect Automatoonz from these security risks.

## Security Controls

There are three types of security controls in AWS, as shown in Figure 3-1: preventive, corrective, and detective. AWS offers misconfiguration detection services like SecurityHub, GuardDuty, and Config. While these are valuable, they are all *detective security controls*: they only detect misconfigurations *after* a resource is created.

It's also important to have *preventive controls* to *prevent* the developers from launching misconfigured resources. Time is the bad actor's best friend: the longer a misconfigured resource is up, the more time they have to poke around the account to find weak points, run different attacks, and gain access to sensitive data.

The third kind of security control is *corrective controls*, which fixes a misconfiguration to bring the system back to its known good state. Developers should aim to have all three controls in place to secure their IaC. In the context of Automatoonz, we will focus on implementing preventive controls and automation first, then detective controls.

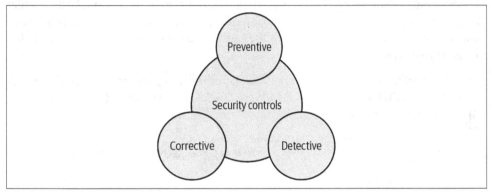

*Figure 3-1. Different types of security controls*

The design goal is to automatically trigger deployments when IaC is pushed to the CodeCommit repository. The workflow will begin with Automatoonz developers committing their code. A commit invokes a build stage, which only deploys into the VPC if the code is up to security standards and considered safe. In the build stage, the security standards and expectations are codified in the form of checks. If the code passes these checks, it is deployed into the environment.

The Automatoonz developers (Aisha and Dave) already have a VPC and associated subnets set up, and have built security groups and other resources to meet their needs. However, what they build is not always secure, which has led to some uncomfortable conversations with the security team.

The developers are using an existing CodeCommit repository to store their code. This will be the starting point for their DevSecOps journey. Having versioned IaC helps the team collaborate on code, roll back deployments, and integrate with testing functions. The developers can integrate their unit tests in the pipeline (which we'll demonstrate later in this and other chapters) to enhance automation and debugging.

However, it emerges that *someone* has created a security group that has port 22 access, open to the internet. This is a problem: bad actors could find this port and use it as an attack vector to brute-force their way into Automatoonz's AWS VPC network. What should the teams do?

Ideally, they should monitor the main branch, since the code there has been merged after human approval and/or reviews. When someone commits code to the Code-Commit repository, a pipeline is executed. As part of this pipeline, the team can select the exact branch they want to monitor for changes. Let's create the pipeline to do that.

# Better Than a Cure: Implementing Preventive Controls

A *pipeline* (as defined by Red Hat (*https://oreil.ly/ukqpA*)) is a "set of steps which must be performed to create a new version of the application"—which, in this case, is Automatoonz's IaC. Follow along with the steps described here to set up your pipeline using AWS developer tools.

To begin, you'll need to set up your CodeCommit repository. You can find the code in the book's GitHub repository (*https://oreil.ly/SaCgh*) (as *ch3-codecommitrepo.yml*), but we'll reproduce it here as well:

```
AWSTemplateFormatVersion: "2010-09-09"
  Description: Template to create CodeCommit repository, CodePipeline
  Parameters:
   CodeCommitName:
     Type: String
     Default: AutomatoonzRepo

  Resources:
   CodecommitRepo:
     Type: AWS::CodeCommit::Repository
     Properties:
       RepositoryName: !Ref CodeCommitName
       RepositoryDescription: Repo created for Automatoonz team infra code
       Tags:
         - Key: Team
           Value: Automatoonz
```

Running this code sets up a CodeCommit repository with the default name AutomatoonzRepo. (If you want to change your repository name, you can do so while launching the CloudFormation stack or pass parameters in the command below.) This is a new, empty repository. As we progress through the steps, you'll add more functionalities into this configuration file to deploy different resources.

To deploy the repository, run this command:

```
> aws cloudformation create-stack \
    --stack-name devsecops-repo \
    --template-body file://ch3-codecommitrepo.yml
```

Use the following command to check its deployment status through the AWS console or the CLI:

```
> aws codecommit list-repositories

{
  "repositories": [
    {
      "repositoryName": "devsecops-repo"
      "repositoryId": "a0000e13-x83x-4027-aaef-650c0XXXXXX",
    }
  ]
}
```

Wait for the repository to launch successfully before moving on.

Next, you'll want to add your first file into the repository. Start by cloning your repository to your local system by executing the steps provided in the AWS documentation (*https://oreil.ly/CoQHU*).

In the root of your cloned repository, create a folder named *cfn* and, in it, create a new file named *secgroup.yml*. The file in the book's repository, *chapter-3/ch3-secgroup.yml*, will have the following contents:

```
AWSTemplateFormatVersion: "2010-09-09"
  Description: Template to create misconfigured security group in a VPC
  Parameters:
   VPCId:
     Type: String

  Resources:
   MisconfiguredSecGroup:
     Type: AWS::EC2::SecurityGroup
     Properties:
       GroupDescription: Misconfigured security group which should NEVER be
           launched
       GroupName: MisconfiguredSecGroup
       SecurityGroupIngress:
         - IpProtocol: tcp
           FromPort: 22
           ToPort: 22
           CidrIp: 0.0.0.0/0
       VpcId: !Ref VPCId
```

This code creates a misconfigured security group with an ingress rule that allows anyone on the internet to use SSH over port 22—just like the one our friends at Automatoonz are dealing with. Let's see how you can stop this group from launching.

# Implementation

Commit the *ch3-secgroup.yml* file to the newly created repository, then push to origin. (As we mentioned at the beginning of this chapter, if you are not familiar with using Git branches, please see *Head First Git* (*https://oreil.ly/T66I1*) or the Git documentation site (*https://oreil.ly/qgpjg*) for help getting started.) You should now be able to see your file in the repository.

You want your commits to trigger the deployment check and only allow deployment if the code is secure, as shown in Figure 3-2.

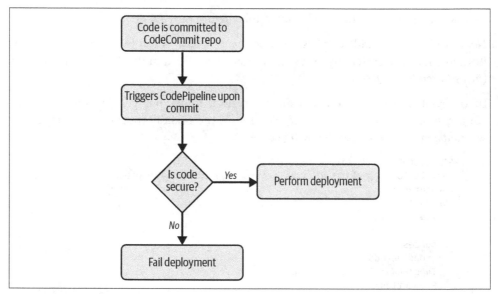

*Figure 3-2. Flow of deployment check*

To achieve this automated deployment check, you will use AWS CodePipeline and AWS CodeBuild. CodePipeline will act as a "harness" to link the phases of the pipeline together, while CodeBuild will be your build, configuration, and testing system. Figure 3-3 represents the full setup.

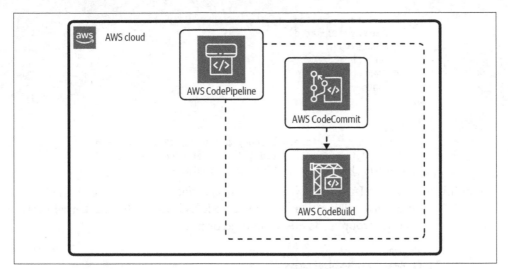

*Figure 3-3. Full setup using AWS CodePipeline and AWS CodeBuild*

You will create another version of the CloudFormation file with CodePipeline and CodeBuild. Let's walk through some snippets of that code. The full version is in the Chapter 3 folder (*https://oreil.ly/M6Rad*) of the book's repository, named *ch3-codepipeline.yml*.

To deploy the file, run this command:

```
> aws cloudformation update-stack \
    --stack-name devsecops-repo \
    --template-body file://ch3-codepipeline.yml \
    --capabilities CAPABILITY_NAMED_IAM
```

In this file, you will see a couple of IAM roles being created. The EventBridge (*https://oreil.ly/2fUuT*) service will use these roles to tell you when someone has committed code to the repository; CodePipeline will use the second role (named CodePipelineRole in the *codepipeline.yml*) to perform tasks on your behalf. The EventBridge rule looks for changes to the CodeCommit repository and triggers CodePipeline whenever someone commits to the main branch. The following excerpt shows the pattern the EventBridge rule is looking for:

```
EventPattern:
      source:
        - aws.codecommit
      detail-type:
        - 'CodeCommit Repository State Change'
      resources:
        - !Join [ '', [ 'arn:aws:codecommit:', !Ref 'AWS::Region', ':',
            !Ref 'AWS::AccountId', ':', !Ref CodecommitRepo ] ]
      detail:
        event:
```

```
             - referenceCreated
             - referenceUpdated
           referenceType:
             - branch
           referenceName:
             - main
         Targets:
           -
           Arn:
             !Join [ '', [ 'arn:aws:codepipeline:', !Ref 'AWS::Region', ':',
                   !Ref 'AWS::AccountId', ':', !Ref CodePipeline ] ]
             RoleArn: !GetAtt AmazonCloudWatchEventRole.Arn
```

In addition to the two IAM roles within *ch3-codepipeline.yml*, you have also created a CodeBuild project that will install an open source IaC checker. The checker will verify whether the security group file is misconfigured or not:

```
CodeBuildProject:
    Type: AWS::CodeBuild::Project
    Properties:
      Name: Automatoonz_Project
      Source:
        Type: CODEPIPELINE
      Description: This project will test Code
      ServiceRole: !GetAtt CodePipelineRole.Arn
      Artifacts:
        Type: CODEPIPELINE
      Environment:
        Type: LINUX_CONTAINER
        ComputeType: BUILD_GENERAL1_SMALL
        Image: aws/codebuild/amazonlinux2-x86_64-standard:2.0
      TimeoutInMinutes: 10
```

The CodeBuild project reads the buildspec file (*buildspec.yml*) from the root directory of the CodeCommit repository during execution. (A buildspec file is a collection of instructions and steps performed in the CodeBuild project; see the AWS documentation (*https://oreil.ly/VilQ5*) for more information.) You'll use this build project as a test stage to check the files you commit into your CodeCommit repo.

The buildspec file performs three major steps. First, it installs an open source checker called cfn-nag (*https://oreil.ly/UOARn*), which scans CloudFormation files. Second, it runs that checker on the code you committed to the repository. Third, it provides a pass or fail result. The next snippet, from the buildspec file, shows the first and second stages:

```
version: 0.2

phases:
  install:
    commands:
      - echo Entering the install phase...
```

```
      - gem install cfn-nag
  build:
    commands:
      - echo Entering the build phase...
      - cfn_nag_scan --input-path $CODEBUILD_SRC_DIR/cfn
```

Now you need to commit *buildspec.yml* to the CodeCommit repository so that the CodeBuild repository can use it.

Once you perform this commit, visit the CodePipeline service in the AWS Management Console. You should see that the pipeline has started its execution (shown in Figure 3-4).

*Figure 3-4. Pipeline running after a new file is committed to the CodeCommit repository*

The first stage of the pipeline is connected to the CodeCommit repository. The pipeline will pull the changes from that repo and pass them on to the next stage, which is the CodeBuild project.

After the build process completes, the pipeline will fail. This is totally normal and expected. This pipeline should fail when there's a misconfigured resource, like the security group you just committed. But how can you know that the pipeline failed for *this* reason and not some other reason?

This is a great time to dive into the pipeline's logs to see what error occurred, and when and where it happened. Within the AWS console, go to CodePipeline and click on the pipeline you just created. TestStage should show as "failed." Click the Details link inside the TestStage box (see Figure 3-5).

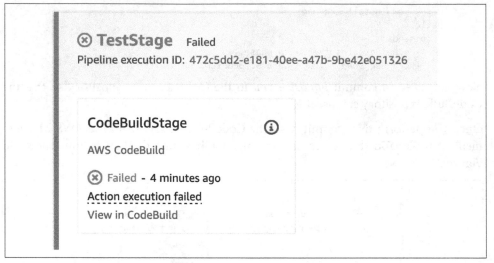

*Figure 3-5. Investigating the error in CodePipeline*

This link will take you to the execution logs from your last run, so you can see what was executed as your stages ran through the pipeline. It should look similar to the following snippet:

```
[Container] 2022/03/23 23:36:50 Running command cfn_nag_scan --input-path
  $CODEBUILD_SRC_DIR
  ------------------------------------------------------------
  /codebuild/output/src699107553/src/secgroup.yml
  ------------------------------------------------------------
  | WARN W28
  |
  | Resource: ["MisconfiguredSecGroup"]
  | Line Numbers: [9]
  |
  | Resource found with an explicit name, this disallows updates that require
  replacement of this resource
  ------------------------------------------------------------
  | WARN W9
  |
  | Resource: ["MisconfiguredSecGroup"]
  | Line Numbers: [9]
  |
  | Security Groups found with ingress cidr that is not /32
  ------------------------------------------------------------
  | WARN W2
  |
  | Resource: ["MisconfiguredSecGroup"]
  | Line Numbers: [9]
  |
  | Security Groups found with cidr open to world on ingress.  This should never
  be true on instance.  Permissible on ELB
```

```
---------------------------------------------------------
| FAIL F1000
|
| Resource: ["MisconfiguredSecGroup"]
| Line Numbers: [9]
|
| Missing egress rule means all traffic is allowed outbound.  Make this
explicit if it is desired configuration
---------------------------------------------------------
| WARN W36
|
| Resource: ["MisconfiguredSecGroup"]
| Line Numbers: [9]
|
| Security group rules without a description obscure their purpose and may lead
to bad practices in ensuring they only allow traffic from the ports and
sources/destinations required.

Failures count: 1
Warnings count: 4

[Container] 2022/03/23 23:36:50 Command did not exit successfully
cfn_nag_scan --input-path $CODEBUILD_SRC_DIR exit status 2
```

As you can see in the logs, the sections that start with `WARN` and `FAIL` are the misconfigurations within your CloudFormation file. The failure occurred because the *secgroup.yml* file had multiple security violations. The security group has the following two warnings and one error:

- `WARN W2`: IP range is open to the world
- `FAIL F1000`: Missing egress rule
- `WARN W36`: Missing security group description

# Summary

In this chapter, you created a CodeCommit repository, a CodePipeline, and a CodeBuild project. When you make a commit to the CodeCommit repository, the CodePipeline gets triggered. The CodePipeline has a CodeBuild project as a stage containing `cfn-nag`, which is a CloudFormation checker.

You learned about three types of security controls that work in tandem to secure your environment, and that adding preventive checks into the software development life cycle as early as possible helps to prevent security events. You also learned that if you control the ingress point where code gets deployed, you can control whether to deploy a given IaC file into your environment.

Understanding logging and errors can help you cut down on bugs and have a successful build. Scanners like `cfn-nag` let you isolate misconfigurations as specific lines of your code, which you can fix before deployment.

The Automatoonz team is off to a great start. They (and you) have created an initial pipeline for conducting IaC checks and preventing security misconfigurations early in the life cycle. In the next chapter, we will show you how to further refine this pipeline by adding logging and monitoring features to detect and prevent tampering.

A quick recap of key takeaways from this chapter:

- There are three types of security controls that developers should have in place to secure IaC: preventive, detective, and corrective.
- When you set up a CodePipeline, preventive checks are triggered when code is committed.
- The open source checker `cfn-nag` will look for common security misconfigurations within code.

# CHAPTER 4

# Logging and Monitoring

Even though Automatoonz has gone through the process of securing its infrastructure, as you saw in the previous chapter, malicious actors will still try to infiltrate its environments. There are different layers to a website, and gaining visibility and awareness in all of them can be complicated. How can they add more safeguards?

In this chapter, we're going to review different threats and attack styles. We'll also look at how proper logging and monitoring techniques can help to implement a *Defense in Depth* strategy, in which multiple or additional security layers are applied to protect an organization and its assets from security vulnerabilities. We'll show you some security tools to protect your organization's endpoints, data, applications, and networks; to stop cyber threats before they happen; and to slow or minimize additional damage in affected areas. Amazon's CloudWatch service, for example, simplifies the collection of operational data and monitoring in the form of logs, metrics, events, and dashboards.

## What Are Logging and Monitoring—and Why Do They Matter?

First, let's clarify some terms. Logging and monitoring are often confused. *Logging* is the act of capturing the information the system or application outputs, while *monitoring* is the act of using the logs to track meaningful events. *Metrics* are specific benchmark measures used to evaluate performance and are an important part of monitoring. *Dashboards* are interfaces that allow users to see everything they are monitoring in one place.

Why do logging and monitoring matter? Logging and monitoring play key roles in any cloud native security strategy. In fact, they are critical to mitigating any gaps in your network's *security visibility* (a strategy for using logs to enhance your understanding of the security environment).

*Observability* is the process of evaluating the state of a system by using logs, metrics, and traces. It is a proactive step in detecting vulnerabilities in your system *before* an attack. You need to be able to observe what's going on in your system and to correlate events and modifications with users. This way, you can spot unknown or anomalous patterns of activity and investigate them before an attack brings down the system.

For example, one metric might be an aggregate where you factor in the event, resource attributes, and timespan. When you take the information in an event and break down the contexts, you'll find that unique static and dynamic relationships start to take shape, and you can standardize on common data structures. This might include using JSON for extracting raw text from records, developing a standard schema for your fields, or using standard libraries, like the Logging module for Python. Avoid logging cryptic or nondescriptive messages that people will have a hard time understanding. Keep logs simple and concise to make them easier to parse.

Meaningful correlations in your data structures can reduce your mean time to restore (the time it takes to recover from a product or system failure) by removing the need to dig through multiple relevant log types across systems and connect alerts with events. Coming up with those meaningful correlations gives you the opportunity to evaluate which events and attributes are just noise and which can provide insights into decoupled activities in the environment.

Filtering the streams of information found in logs is equally valuable, and also difficult without the proper mechanisms in place that logging and monitoring features offer. Understanding different attacks that can be used is critical in identifying patterns that emerge.

# Attack Styles

The style of an attack will depend on the attacker's goals and whether they are playing the "long game" or not. For instance, ransomware programs automatically spread through infected networks, which is a direct short-term attack. But ransomware has been evolving into different types. In *human-operated ransomware* attacks, the attackers gather as much information as possible about their target, often waiting months before launching an attack. Sophisticated attacks like this can cause key industries and infrastructure, like oil pipelines and healthcare, to halt operations for hours or even weeks.

# Advanced Persistent Threat Attacks

The evolution in ransomware (although morally bankrupt) has led to an increase in extortion ransomware and ransomware as a service (RaaS). These are known as *advanced persistent threat* (APT) attacks. Here are some broad classifications:

*Crypto-ransomware*
> Allows attackers to access devices and encrypt all of the data or objects, rendering them useless without the decryption key from the attacker. Crypto-ransomware confronts users with a screen demanding payment that includes a counter or deadline. If the victim doesn't pay by the deadline, the encrypted data is permanently deleted.

*Leakware or doxware*
> Threatens to release confidential or sensitive data if the ransom is not paid in time. Typical targets include financial institutions and public companies.

*Locker ransomware*
> Locks the victim out of their systems and limits their abilities; they can only interact with screens related to the ransom demands. This attack also restricts the functioning of peripherals, like keyboards and mice. Most of the time, locker ransomware doesn't *destroy* data on the target system, but rather blocks the victim from accessing the data. Usually, a countdown or timer is displayed to pressure the victim to pay.

*Ransomware as a service (RaaS)*
> Enables malicious actors with little or no technical knowledge or programming skill to subscribe to a SaaS-like business model in order to deploy a ransomware attack. The RaaS provider takes a percentage of the ransom in payment for providing the service.

*Man-in-the-middle (MitM)*
> Secretly relays (and possibly modifies) communications between two legitimate parties to an illegitimate third party inserted between them. The two unsuspecting legitimate parties believe they are communicating with each other directly. This is a form of eavesdropping that involves intercepting information and data from both parties while also sending malicious links or other information to both legitimate participants, potentially allowing the attacker to impersonate one of the parties to gain access to their systems.

*Privilege escalation*
> Elevates the attacker's access at the application, database, or even operating system level. For example, if a security compromise occurred where a bad actor elevated their privilege to remove a key component of a service, this could cause major disruption to that service.

We'll discuss APT attacks more in Chapter 6.

## Ransomware Strains

Now, let's look at a few examples of specific ransomware strains:

*CryptoLocker*
> In this locker ransomware strain, the malicious attacker encrypts the victim's data. The victim has to pay for the private key to decrypt their data in order to regain access. Payment is generally demanded in the form of Bitcoin or prepaid vouchers, to reduce traceability. If the victim misses the deadline, the ransomware deletes the private key, permanently denying access to the encrypted data. CryptoLocker targets Microsoft operating systems and is delivered via an email attachment.

*Bad Rabbit*
> In this strain, the victim's system file tables are encrypted. Its code contains string values consisting of character names from the TV series *Game of Thrones*. The payment demand is in the form of Bitcoin. It targets Microsoft operating systems and uses compromised websites to spread a fake Adobe Flash update as the delivery method.

*Cerber*
> This RaaS attack targets cloud-based Microsoft 365 users. A password-protected, zipped *.DOT* file is hidden in malicious ads or suspicious emails. It contains a macro or Windows Script File that infects the victim's local host. The payment demand is in the form of Bitcoin.

## Passive and Active Attacks

*Passive attackers* typically attempt to access sensitive or business-critical data through any endpoints or applications authenticated to the target organization's network. They infect the endpoints with malware, leaving the data intact. The attacker discreetly monitors the victim's system and network by analyzing transfer rates and connectivity levels, scanning for open ports, recording ingress and egress traffic, and collecting information from communication channels in the victim's environment. The attacker uses that information to identify vulnerabilities they can exploit to plan and perform attacks.

For example, a passive attacker might exploit an expired certificate on a security device. The 2017 Equifax data breach (*https://oreil.ly/TVI3Z*) was conducted in this fashion; the attackers used a packet analyzer tool to monitor network traffic. It installed a keylogger and waited for users to enter their credentials, which it recorded for later use.

*Active attackers* gain unauthorized access and cause damage to a network's performance. For instance, they can delete, modify, corrupt, de-encrypt, and re-encrypt data with different keys. Often, active attackers use a combination of attack types to layer on complexity with advanced persistent threats. Some examples of active attacks include:

*Code and SQL injection*

This attack is often used on websites to steal or destroy sensitive data from organizations or end users. *SQL injection,* or inserting SQL queries, is a technique where malicious SQL statements are inserted into input fields, leveraging the existing execution process in a SQL database. The attacker can modify the SQL to return additional results (hidden data). The query can subvert an application's logic, retrieve data from multiple database tables (called union attacks), gather information about the version and schemas of the database (called database exploits), and perform queries that do not return in the application's responses (called blind SQL injections).

*Distributed Denial of Service (DDoS)*

This attack attempts to affect or exhaust the resources available to legitimate users of a target's website, network, application, or service. Internet of Things (IoT) botnets or devices can create a volumetric DDoS attack, using their traffic to overload a system's network. The attack can compromise the application layer by starving backend resources, or encrypted traffic can cause floods on your networks, known as SSL DDoS attacks. As with ransomware, there's also a market for DDoS as a service.

*Cross-site scripting (XSS)*

This attack injects or inserts malicious client-side code into the code of a trusted application or website. The attacker sends malicious links in hopes that the victim will open them, allowing the attacker's code to run on the victim's local system. The attacker can then steal the victim's active session cookie or session token. This compromises account access, since the attacker can impersonate the victim. The injected code can record keystrokes, redirect users to unintended websites, and expose sensitive site-specific information. Web browser–based exploits can also disrupt the user experience by crashing the browser.

*Unauthorized access*

This attack can occur any time an external or internal actor gains access without authorization to data, networks, endpoints, applications, systems, or devices.

This isn't a complete list, but it should give you an idea of the breadth of the potential attacks you need to prepare for. Next, we'll look more closely at log types and logging, which can detect not only security breaches and attacks, but also operational issues.

# Log Types

Infrastructure is the sum of multiple components, both physical and virtual: software, virtual machines, virtual servers, virtual networks, and so forth. The log files from these components are known as *infrastructure logs*. AWS provides software monitoring agents to capture infrastructure logs from systems, hardware devices, networks, and user activities. The logged information could contain timestamps for events in different standardized formats (depending on the configuration), universally unique identifiers (UUIDs), event sources and destinations, and additional data. People or machine-driven algorithms can analyze collected infrastructure logs. They can query or sort aggregates and view new relationships to detect operational issues, as well as to identify security breaches or malicious attacks by internal or external actors.

*Application logs* are composed of the data generated by software applications running on nodes, EC2 instances, or containers. Applications deployed on the infrastructure also constitute a potential attack plane on the presentation layer. The nature of these attacks is likely to differ based on the written codebase's programming language (such as Python, Go, or Java), so that's a good starting point for deciding which attacks your detection tools should look for.

Application logging can identify vulnerabilities that can be introduced in many ways: by legacy libraries in applications, data management, systemic issues, the development life cycle, and even proper testing, token, and certification rotation in the environment. For example, an attacker might extend the time range of a session ID that stores information about when an application's authentication expires. This gives them time to explore the target environment, escalate access privileges, or even attempt to brute-force their way through weak patterns.

In addition to generating infrastructure and application logs, you can use tools for further analysis, including:

*Security information event management (SIEM) tools*
> SIEM tools can further analyze and correlate logs to help identify any security compromises.

*Dashboard tools*
> Dashboards use log data to create visuals, such as graphs and tables, that help people identify patterns or anomalies that could indicate a security compromise.

*Incident management tools*
> Incident management tools allow support personnel to review the logs, triage problems during incidents, and actively resolve issues. In addition, these tools can archive logs and use them to perform root cause analysis.

As you can see, analyzing logs requires storing them safely. Let's look at log storage next.

# Log Storage

In the latest Amazon Linux images (as of fall 2022), the `amazon-cloudwatch-agent` package is available for installation. It will create a predefined JSON configuration file (*https://oreil.ly/gEjiV*) and user `cwagent` during installation. You can also access the console by running the following command:

```
> sudo /opt/aws/amazon-cloudwatch-agent/bin/amazon-cloudwatch-agent-config-wizard
```

The system will then prompt you for information and an AWS Systems Manager (SSM) document. There is an option to customize the CloudWatch agent username, proxy settings, and metrics by manually editing the configuration file (*/opt/aws/amazon-cloudwatch-agent/bin/config.json*) and reloading the latest changes:

```
> sudo /opt/aws/amazon-cloudwatch-agent/bin/amazon-cloudwatch-agent-ctl \
-a fetchconfig -m ec2 \
-c file:/opt/aws/amazon-cloudwatch-agent/bin/config.json -s
```

The last step is to develop an IAM role for the EC2 instance that has the CloudWatch-AgentServerPolicy attached.

This allows infrastructure metrics to be extended to `openldap`, `openvpn`, packet filtering, syslog, and so forth. Application access and error logs can be sent to CloudWatch as individual log streams, based on the source.

> The latest (as of this writing) CloudWatch agents support StatsD (*https://oreil.ly/zSGoD*) and collectd (*https://oreil.ly/6E33e*) daemons and AWS OpenTelemetry (*https://oreil.ly/LKLPK*). OpenTelemetry enables applications with OpenTelemetry metrics to integrate with CloudWatch. It is supported by CloudWatch Embedded Metric Format (EMF) (*https://oreil.ly/EouW2*).

During the CloudWatch agent configuration, CloudWatch logs enable you to store all customer metrics from the previous 14 days for up to 15 months. By default, the service uses aging logic to roll up logs together for longer periods of storage. For example, data that is stored at 1-minute resolution will be rolled up into data points at 5-minute resolution after 15 days. That window will continue to increase, up to one hour after a set number of days, unless the logs are offloaded to different storage solutions (see Example 4-1).

*Example 4-1. Code snippet from AWS SSM document to configure a CloudWatch agent using IaC*

```
Resources:
  CloudWatchConfigParameter:
    DependsOn: EC2Instance
    Type: AWS::SSM::Parameter
```

```
Properties:
  Name: AmazonCloudWatch-linux
  Type: String
  Value: !Sub |
    {
      "agent": {
        "metrics_collection_interval": 60,
        "run_as_user": "cwagent"
      },
      "logs": {
        "logs_collected": {
          "files": {
            "collect_list": [
              {
                "file_path": "/var/log/nginx/error.log",
                "log_group_name": "DemoApp/error.log",
                "log_stream_name": "{EC2Instance}"
              },
              {
                "file_path": "/var/log/nginx/access.log",
                "log_group_name": "DemoApp/access.log",
                "log_stream_name": "{EC2Instance}"
              }
            ]
          }
        }
      }
    }
```

To preserve the original data resolution and to meet possible compliance require-ments, you can store logs in different Amazon S3 bucket types, where CloudWatch log rollup does not automatically apply and manual rollup is required. You can define life cycle rules to automatically migrate Amazon S3 objects to S3 Standard-Infrequent Access (Standard-IA), Amazon S3 Glacier Instant Retrieval, Amazon S3 Glacier Flexible Retrieval, or Amazon S3 Glacier Deep Archive, based on the age or number of newer versions of the data. (For more information on Amazon S3, see the official AWS documentation (*https://oreil.ly/3F0Ki*).)

You can also set life cycle policies by bucket, prefix, object tags, or object size, allowing you to delete data at its end of life. The advantage of life cycle rules and policies is that they help reduce the cost of storage by either archiving the data to lower-cost storage or deleting data that is no longer needed.

Defining life cycle rules can be tedious and time-consuming, however. To avoid this, consider using Amazon S3 Intelligent-Tiering service (Figure 4-1). According to its documentation (*https://oreil.ly/fLf9L*), this service "automatically moves objects that have not been accessed to lower-cost access tiers," without operational overhead or data deletion. Then, you can enable versioning of sensitive or operation-critical logs to maintain their integrity and make it easier to recover from a disaster.

Figure 4-1 shows this workflow, with the following steps:

1. The EC2 instance is streaming log data to CloudWatch logs.
2. AWS Lambda is invoked when there is log data waiting to be written.
3. AWS Lambda pushes the logs into an S3 bucket for storage.
4. All logs are encrypted using S3 server-side encryption.

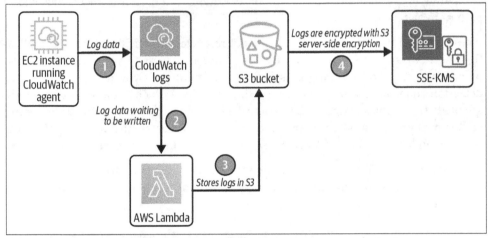

*Figure 4-1. Storing CloudWatch logs from an EC2 instance in an S3 bucket*

By default, CloudWatch logs use server-side encryption for the log data at rest.

Another option for encryption is AWS Key Management Service (KMS). Using a customer-managed KMS key, you can apply encryption at the log group level at the time of provisioning, or after the resource exists. The CloudWatch log decrypts the data upon request, but needs additional permissions for the customer-managed key in such cases. Amazon S3 server-side encryption using KMS (SSE-KMS) can be applied at the bucket level. S3 will only share an S3 bucket key for objects encrypted by the same KMS key. To configure an S3 bucket key for existing objects, you can use a COPY operation. This will reduce calls from S3 to KMS, in turn reducing traffic to these services.

The KMS key does not retroactively encrypt data that was added before the key was applied. It only encrypts new log data that arrives after the key is applied.

# Detecting Anomalies

You can transform the ingested data from CloudWatch logs into metric filters. *Metric filters* contain a set of key elements: default value, dimensions, filter pattern, metric name, and metric value. To create alarms and visual representations, you can turn the metric filters into numerical CloudWatch metrics. This is where you can make use of CloudWatch's anomaly detection feature. *Anomalies* are data points that are irregular compared to the rest of the dataset, or deviations from some normal behavioral pattern in a given time frame.

Anomalies can happen anywhere; they're not restricted to infrastructure and application logs. Say a malicious actor is attempting to gain access to your web application by scanning and brute-forcing passwords for usernames. If you don't have anomaly detection enabled, you might not notice this intrusion, which could have dire consequences. Important customer data could be compromised. You could lose control of business-critical services, or an outage could take down the whole application, resulting in lost revenue and leaving your team scrambling to restore service.

Your monitoring automations should cover all available data streams, because bad actors leave no stone unturned. The benefits of investing in automated anomaly detection tools include:

- Finding out about customer-facing issues *before* the customer experiences any service degradation or interruption
- Reducing the time needed to identify the root cause of an anomaly
- Reducing the need to correlate data from different sources manually
- Gaining valuable insights into your operations, which can be used for improvement and future feature development
- Proactive monitoring for security and regulatory compliance, without overloading operations staff with too many different dashboards to watch

Anomaly detection is sometimes included in compliance requirements. For example, some fintech companies are required by regulations to use anomaly detection with end-to-end synthetic transaction capabilities. This requirement allows them to generate and test different synthetic transaction scenarios to produce various anomaly situations. The synthetic transactions are simulating activity normally performed in an application or on a website by a real person.

> Metric math (*https://oreil.ly/iPf1z*) uses statistical techniques to detect and calculate behaviors in datasets. This helps data scientists teach machine learning algorithms to detect anomalies.

Anomaly detection tools use machine learning to perform versatile pattern matching, similar to regular expressions. The filter pattern element uses alphanumeric and nonalphanumeric characters, operators, and case sensitivity. For example, in an application's web server access logs, you might create a metric filter called 4xxCount to extract individual log events, which produces metric values for all HTTP 4xx error codes. Gathering this metric data provides a means to identify HTTP 4xx error code patterns.

You can use metric filters in combination with CloudWatch alarms to monitor metrics, for example 4xxCount, and respond to changes (see Example 4-2). For example, you could set an alarm to alert you any time 4xxCount changes, shortening the time to discovery.

*Example 4-2. Code snippet from file ch4_cloudwatchlog-alarm.yml to create a CloudWatch metric filter*

```
CWLogMetricFilter:
  DependsOn: CWLogGroup
  Type: AWS::Logs::MetricFilter
  Properties:
    FilterPattern: !Ref LogFilterPattern
    LogGroupName: !Ref CWLogGroup
    MetricTransformations:
    -
        MetricValue: !Ref LogFilterMetricValue
        MetricNamespace: !Ref LogFilterMetricName
        MetricName: !Ref LogFilterMetricName
```

In AWS CloudTrail, you can customize filters and alarms to watch billing trends and alert you when an unusual or excessive number of resources are provisioned or taken down in an account. This can help you detect issues such as forgotten resources, compromised user access, and overly permissioned roles in teams and organizations. Let's look to Automatoonz for an example.

As you've seen in the previous chapters, Automatoonz has been deploying resources at breakneck speed. The development, security, and finance teams need to monitor multiple dimensions. Although funding has not been an issue, some managers (especially Linda) have been raising eyebrows at the consistently increasing costs of the AWS accounts. Linda asks Ravi, a DevSecOps engineer, to find out where the overspending is coming from.

Ravi logs into the AWS console and creates a Cost and Usage Report in CloudTrail. This shows him which resource types, regions, and tags have been accruing bills. Since Automatoonz works in a single US region, he decides to create alerts based on the tags and regions to track and alert the team when there is unauthorized activity across unapproved regions.

While reviewing the billing data, Ravi notices billing activities for resources in a US region that should be disabled, according to company policy. He knows it's possible to disable a region and still have resources there that continue to incur charges. He checks to see if logging is enabled for that US region in CloudTrail (it isn't) and if any logs are stored for it (there aren't). Ravi shows the operations team his findings and asks for permission to access and explore these mysterious instances and the applications they've been running.

Upon investigating the should-be-disabled region, Ravi finds a small Discord setup mimicking a local SIP provider that offers international telephone service. This fraudulent setup has been attempting to record sessions and steal data. Ravi writes a root cause analysis (RCA) report with the details, and new engineer Jake works quickly to decommission the unauthorized resources. The security team follows up by using IaC to set monitoring alarms, dashboards, Config rules, and proper logging so that this won't happen again.

CloudTrail is great for investigating API activity in an AWS account, but for a more granular view of your application's behavior and events, CloudWatch can output custom information. CloudWatch's anomaly detection feature can analyze past metric data for statistics and anomaly thresholds, then create a model of expected values. In the dashboard shown in Figure 4-2, you can visualize hourly, daily, and weekly patterns in the metric data. You can even perform calculations using math expressions with `GetMetricData`, then create new time series based on these metrics. This is useful for detecting APT attacks.

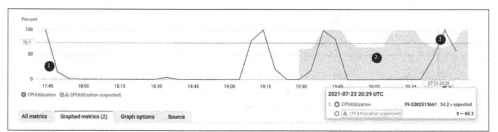

*Figure 4-2. A CPU usage spike detected in a CloudWatch dashboard widget*

We can see the following in Figure 4-2:

1. The line in the graph represents the normal data flow.
2. The envelope or band around the data is the configured or allowed threshold within which the normal data is expected to fluctuate.
3. The line outside the band represents the abnormal pattern detected in that time frame.

You can also detect anomalies with updates to dashboards, which serve as a visual aid to investigate events further.

As a best practice, when creating an anomaly detector, configure the following in Example 4-3:

*Example 4-3. CloudWatch alarm with anomaly detection for a Java application's memory (code snippet from file ch4_cloudwatchlog-alarm.yml)*

```
CWAnomalyDetectorOnUsedMemory:
  Type: 'AWS::CloudWatch::AnomalyDetector'
  Properties:
    MetricName: !Ref AnomalyMetricName ❶
    Namespace: !Ref AnomalyNameSpace
    Stat: !Ref AnomalyStat
    Dimensions: ❷
      - Name: !Ref AnomalyDimName
        Value: !Ref AnomalyDimValue
    Configuration:
      MetricTimeZone: !Ref AnomalyConfigZone
      ExcludedTimeRanges:
        - StartTime: !Ref AnomalyConfigExcludeStart
          EndTime: !Ref AnomalyConfigExcludeEnd
```

❶ CloudWatch metric to watch.

❷ Dimension name and value. These fields are optional, but the value creates the threshold criteria for the anomaly detector to generate a CloudWatch alarm.

Understanding metric data and time series aggregations can be complex. It's important to contextualize your information. If you make decisions with limited data or data from the wrong time bracket, you might make incorrect decisions. When in doubt, zoom out and look at the bigger picture, with bigger units of time. Let's consider another example.

Since Automatoonz sells video games, there's a seasonal flow to its site traffic that maps to the demographics of its customer base. For instance, in September, media entertainment traffic and sales tend to decrease because of school starting. The company also holds holiday-driven sale events. Thus, Automatoonz's usage of EC2 instances ebbs and flows in patterns throughout the year. As the company gathers more historical data and sees patterns emerge, its anomaly detection efforts become more accurate.

When the AWS bill reflects a spike in usage, Ravi, the DevSecOps engineer, asks around. None of the dev team members have noticed a spike in the EC2 resource usage graphs. Ravi notices that they're only looking at data from the past week, so he tries graphing the data over a period of weeks, then months. Now everyone can see the spike. It turns out that some of the developers have been leaving their EC2 instances on without using them.

Ravi shows his observations to Dave, the dev team lead, who promises to investigate how to improve the team's resource management. The two of them agree to refine the IaC values in their monitoring to reduce notifications for false alerts or alarms. Because the code has been committed to a version-controlled repository, they can automate management of these configuration changes using a pipeline.

## Remediation with AWS Config

AWS Config and CloudWatch also provide other managed services that can evaluate CloudFormation configurations, record changes over time, provide historical records for audits, and perform security analyses on AWS resources.

AWS Config, for instance, allows you to codify policy and guidelines for your environment and to receive notifications whenever a resource's configuration drifts from the associated rules. It is a service you have to enable in your environment to record configurations, which can take some time to complete. For more information on AWS Config, see the official documentation (*https://oreil.ly/FJ6ne*).

If AWS Config detects noncompliant resources, it notifies you and provides programmatic auto-remediation actions to get them back into compliance, without you having to set up additional monitoring. AWS Config also evaluates your existing configuration against the latest policy changes, to keep the system up to date and minimize technical debt.

 If AWS Config detects multiple resource dependencies that could cause errors, you can use it to preview direct and indirect relationships. For example, the relationship between an EC2 instance and a security group is a direct relationship, because security groups are returned as part of the "describe API" response for an EC2 instance. However, the relationship between a security group and EC2 is an indirect relationship, because EC2 instances are not returned as part of the "describe API" response for a security group.

Keep in mind that AWS Config has configuration records from your account's entire history, which it can leverage to compare or troubleshoot resource issues. You can send the configuration history and snapshots to existing or new S3 buckets, depending on your organization's policies for centralized logging. This gives you historical data that can help reduce the time to a solution or technical debt. You can also enable configuration changes and notifications to an existing or new Simple Notification Service (SNS) topic as a form of alert across accounts in the same region.

As the resources in your AWS account go through provision and depreciation cycles, you can use AWS Config rules to evaluate resources across the account, including:

- Enforcing encryption on EC2 volumes
- Ensuring CloudTrail is enabled for logging
- Checking that VPC security groups are only open to authorized ports

These are part of a list of AWS Config managed rules, modeled after common best practices, that can be predefined or customized. The managed rules can be found under the Config service within the AWS console. To add custom AWS Config rules, you can develop them using Custom Config Rules or Custom Lambda Rules (programming languages supported by AWS Lambda), then add them to AWS Config.

There are three types of actions that can invoke an AWS Config rule: making a change in the AWS resource, changing the schedule, and invoking a rule through the console. There are two kinds of remediation actions associated with invoking an AWS Config rule: manual (not recommended) and automatic (recommended). A remediation action is invoked by an AWS Systems Manager API and a configuration file that contains the details of the tasks to perform to return to compliant status. Let's look at the two kinds:

*Manual remediation*

A manual remediation action might be something like a person updating a noncritical software package (say, updating bash from version 3.0 to version 5.1.16) in waves across EC2 instances to be compliant with Linux nodes.

*Automatic remediation*

Automatic remediation actions happen when an AWS Config rule evaluates the state of a resource and finds it to be noncompliant. If auto-remediation is enabled, AWS Config invokes the SSM APIs to run the SSM configuration file. For example, you could enable S3 bucket encryption with the preconfigured SSM configuration file *AWS-EnableS3BucketEncryption*, or develop your own configuration file in JSON or YAML format for custom operations to start existing workflows. To streamline processes, this might mean invoking a notification via email or webhook to create a ticket in your IT service management tool.

AWS Config rule evaluations will run based on tags associated with the resources. A good tagging system can reduce unnecessary noise and streamline processes. Chapter 5 will discuss tagging in more detail.

Over time, AWS Config rules can become monotonous to manage because you need to create them individually for each region and account. AWS Config's *conformance packs* are collections of rules and remediation actions at a higher, more abstract layer. This feature simplifies organization-wide deployment and compliance reporting by summarizing compliant and noncompliant resources. You can then drill down as needed for details.

When you deploy a conformance pack to an organization's main (parent class) account, the pack becomes immutable. Member (child class) accounts cannot delete or modify the information. This can prevent development teams from disabling the baseline checks needed for governance. It also streamlines configuration rules and simplifies deployment across AWS organizations within a region.

You can use AWS Config's *configuration item* feature to track resources outside of AWS. For on-premises nodes, you use a connector—a mechanism designed to "perform transfer of control and data among components."[1] Here, the connector pulls the data and then calls AWS public APIs to stream that data into AWS Config. You can also track and monitor GitHub repositories, whether public or private, and customize, track, monitor, and ensure compliance for resources not currently supported in AWS.

By combining AWS Config rules with EventBridge events and AWS Lambda, you can implement a custom resource that records the configuration of any active directories not natively supported in AWS Config. For example, you could develop a rule that checks all users' password configurations in Active Directory and reports as noncompliant any profiles with "password never expires" set to "true." Figure 4-3 illustrates how this works.

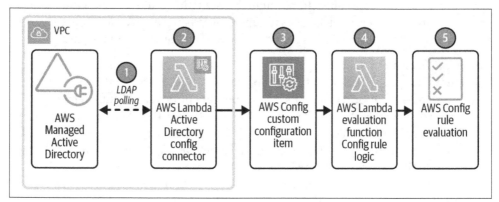

*Figure 4-3. Using existing Active Directory groups and roles to invoke AWS Config rule evaluation*

1 Richard N. Taylor, Nenad Medvidovic, and Eric M. Dashofy, *Software Architecture: Foundations, Theory, and Practice* (John Wiley & Sons, Inc., 2010).

The steps are as follows:

1. LDAP polling retrieves information from Active Directory.
2. AWS Lambda calls the custom Config APIs to create a custom configuration item.
3. The custom configuration item is created.
4. AWS Lambda with the custom Config rule is invoked to perform the evaluation.
5. AWS Config outputs the results of its evaluation.

# Correlating User Activity with CloudTrail

AWS CloudTrail, as we saw earlier, records user activity and API usage across AWS services as events. An *event*, in this context, is a single request from any source and includes information about the requested action, the date and time of the action, the parameters of the request, and so forth, in JSON format. This can help with security monitoring, troubleshooting, and auditing. CloudTrail turns event records into a single trail or multiple trails (depending on the organization) to deliver log files to an Amazon S3 bucket you specify. You can apply filters to events to pinpoint specific activities.

For advanced or complex queries across multiple fields in a CloudTrail event, you can enable CloudTrail Lake, a feature that uses SQL to bring your data into a single, searchable event data store. This allows you to quickly customize information and perform analyses on streaming data. CloudWatch alerts can be set up to detect unauthorized modifications to a security group. Let's see how Automatoonz benefits from using CloudTrail.

Dave, the dev team lead, has been making changes to the security group rules to test his application. Since Dave has permission to add new rules, he is changing rules in ways that have not been approved or reviewed by Ravi's DevSecOps team. This would be fine if Dave was removing the rules he adds after testing, or if those rules were not risky. As of last week, however, Jake, the new DevSecOps engineer, has found 10 instances of port 25 being opened in multiple security groups. It's so bad that Jake is now spending about half of his time just querying and reverting security group rules.

Ravi and Jake sit down to figure out how to reduce this toil. Ravi presents a solution: using CloudWatch event rules, they can set up event-based actions by monitoring CloudTrail events. Now, they'll get alerts any time Dave changes the security group rules, and they can tell Dave to clean up the insecure rules immediately.

Although this is a good first step, there is still room for improvement. After adding the alerting mechanism, Ravi spends some time learning about SSM automation documents, which are a sort of playbook with instructions for setting up actions that tell AWS what to do—in this case, either remove or sink the traffic, so the application isn't exposed.

The flow will look something like this: when Dave edits a security group rule, it triggers a CloudWatch event rule, which starts an SSM automation document, which removes the rule from the security group. Ravi and Jake decide to implement IaC for this process to streamline the work and strengthen standards, readability, accountability, and auditability for the team. This will save Jake time and ensure that nothing is missed because of human error, reducing the risk of security-related exposures or outages.

You can set an alert for any `DeleteSecurityGroup` events. If you get an alert, you'd then open the AWS Management Console, go to "CloudTrail → Event history" and select `DeleteSecurityGroup` to see the event. Example 4-4 shows part of a JSON `DeleteSecurityGroup` event record.

*Example 4-4. Output from a DeleteSecurityGroup JSON event record*

```
{
    "eventVersion": "1.08",
    "userIdentity": {
        "type": "AssumedRole",
        "principalId": "AXXXXXXXXXXXX:username",
        "arn": "arn:aws:sts::12345678910:assumed-role/developer/username",
        "accountId": "12345678910",
        "accessKeyId": "AXXXXXXXXXXXXXXX",
        "sessionContext": {
            "sessionIssuer": {
                "type": "Role",
                "principalId": "AXXXXXXXXXXXXXXX",
                "arn": "arn:aws:iam::12345678910:role/developer",
                "accountId": "12345678910",
                "userName": "developer"
            },
            "webIdFederationData": {},
            "attributes": {
                "creationDate": "2022-07-18T00:00:22Z",
                "mfaAuthenticated": "false"
            }
        }
    },
    "eventTime": "2022-07-18T17:12:29Z",
    "eventSource": "ec2.amazonaws.com",
    "eventName": "DeleteSecurityGroup",
    "awsRegion": "us-region-1",
    "sourceIPAddress": "XXXXXXXXXXX",
```

```
"userAgent": "XXXXXXXXXXX",
"requestParameters": {
    "groupId": "sg-XXXXXXXXXX"
}
```

As this Automatoonz example illustrates, correlating CloudTrail events can be very useful as you triage issues in your cloud environment. This practice reduces the time it takes to perform a root cause analysis and figure out a solution.

# Network Monitoring with an Amazon VPC

Network monitoring can track transfer rates and connectivity levels, and record ingress and egress traffic to profile baselines for your environment. Amazon virtual private clouds (VPCs) (*https://oreil.ly/cfq9C*) are a core resource component that allows you to launch other AWS resources in a virtual network that you've configured. This virtual network is similar to a traditional network in a datacenter, but with the benefits of a native cloud provider. You can further leverage your monitoring and alerting by using a VPC in combination with AWS Config, EventBridge events, CloudWatch alarms, and notifications.

For instance, there's a predefined AWS Config rule for enabling VPC Flow Logs, called `vpc-flow-logs-enabled`. VPC Flow Logs forwards IP traffic going to and from network interfaces in your AWS VPC to a logging mechanism. By default, this feature is disabled due to the volume of data it generates.

Flow logs are another source of data you can use to identify security group and network ACL rules that are too open or closed. For more information about VPC Flow Logs, see the official documentation (*https://oreil.ly/M4SRK*).

The `vpc-flow-logs-enabled` rule tells AWS Config to detect and track the state of a feature and invoke a custom action if required. If there are route modifications, like network ACL changes, or requirements to track source and destination IP traffic flows, you could develop EventBridge events to detect changes and invoke CloudWatch alarms. Flow log data can be published to, and then viewed in and retrieved from, CloudWatch logs or S3. IPV4 and IPV6 protocols are also supported. Figure 4-4 shows this process.

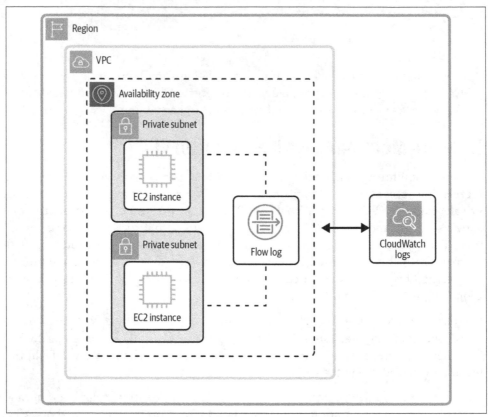

*Figure 4-4. VPC flow logs being streamed to CloudWatch logs for storage*

Security groups are stateful, and you add rules that control the traffic based on protocols and port numbers. The IP address and port information are tracked for all traffic; responses are not tracked as new requests. This allows outbound network traffic for the security group rule without additional configurations. You can apply or change security group associations while launching an instance or after the resources are provisioned.

The *network access control list* (usually called the *network ACL*) is stateless and allows or denies specific inbound or outbound traffic at the subnet level. Egress and ingress traffic must be explicitly allowed by rules that are evaluated in order, starting with the lowest-numbered rule. This automatically applies to all instances in the subnets with which that network ACL is associated. This provides an additional layer of defense if the security group rules are too permissive.

Let's look at an example from the official VPC documentation (*https://oreil.ly/PE8yv*):

> You use the `ping` command from your home computer (IP address is 203.0.113.12) to your instance (the network interface's private IP address is 172.31.16.139). Your security group's inbound rules allow ICMP traffic, but the outbound rules do not allow ICMP traffic. Because security groups are stateful, the response ping from your instance is allowed. Your network ACL permits inbound ICMP traffic, but does not permit outbound ICMP traffic. Because network ACLs are stateless, the response ping is dropped and does not reach your home computer.

To see the network activity in a VPC, you have to enable the VPC Flow Logs feature (which is disabled by default due to the amount of data the network traffic generates). A default flow log displays the following two records:

- An ACCEPT record for the originating ping that was allowed by both the network ACL and the security group, and therefore was allowed to reach your instance:

  ```
  2 123456789010 eni-1235b8ca123456789 203.0.113.12 172.31.16.139 0 0 1 4
  336 1432917027 1432917142 ACCEPT OK
  ```

- A REJECT record for the response ping that the network ACL denied:

  ```
  2 123456789010 eni-1235b8ca123456789 172.31.16.139 203.0.113.12 0 0 1 4
  336 1432917094 1432917142 REJECT OK
  ```

If your network ACL permits outbound ICMP traffic, the flow log displays two ACCEPT records (one for the originating ping and one for the response ping). If your security group denies inbound ICMP traffic, the flow log displays a single REJECT record, because the traffic was not permitted to reach your instance.

The basics of networking and routing still apply to VPCs—they're just part of the managed service, to remove some of the heavy lifting and allow you to focus on innovating.

# Summary

Ultimately, the goal of a DevSecOps engineer is to maintain the health of the business's services and provide a consistent, reliable customer experience (internally and externally) while reducing unnecessary security risk. When unexpected events happen, observability mechanisms enable you to answer questions about what has happened, who is affected, and how to resolve the issue as quickly as possible. Intelligent, intentional logging and monitoring for cloud native architectures can improve resolution time while increasing overall customer satisfaction.

A quick recap of key takeaways from this chapter:

- Logging and monitoring are constant and dynamic exercises. You will need to actively refine your logging, alerts, and alarms.

- It's important to educate yourself on known and emerging threat types and styles. This will allow you to develop methods to detect and prevent threats and attacks against your environments.

- Knowing the different log types allows you to understand where different data is stored and how that information can be accessed. Having this organization helps with data retention, audits, and compliance reviews.

- Understanding the latest AWS managed services and their features will help you make sense of existing and new data. You can leverage automation with code to invoke remediation, reducing the time of exposure or risk.

CHAPTER 5

# Controlling Access Through Automation

In this chapter, we will focus on identity. Specifically, we will discuss enabling authentication and authorization through automation. You will learn about tools you can use to prevent and detect misconfigurations related to identity and access management within your environment.

As a reminder, *authentication* is how you prove who you are, or validate your identity; *authorization* means granting a user permission to do something.

Let's start by thinking about the environment in which you currently work, if applicable. Do you know how many accounts are overly permissive? How many of your permissions are actually used?

There are two types of identities: human and machine. *Human identities* are accounts used by humans for daily, noncritical, or one-off operations. Accounts with *machine identities* are used by machines for automating or carrying out certain privileged operations. In an ideal world, human identities would only be used for reading data that is maintained by machine identities. All operations should be automated as much as possible through machine identities.

In our case study, the members of the Automatoonz DevSecOps team need to provide identities to the users of their infrastructure (humans), as well as to the infrastructure itself (machines). Machine identities will allow services such as EC2 or S3 to communicate with each other. If the infrastructure within AWS does not have the right permissions, you will always get a "Permission Denied" error.

We'll begin the chapter by examining how the principle of least privilege is critical to your information security program. We'll then move on to fine-tuning permissions, covering how to scale IAM permissions with resource tagging and separation of duties. We'll also discuss why prevention is just as important as detection when it comes to IAM security controls. We'll wrap up this chapter by creating a pipeline for detecting IAM policies that are not aligned with security best practices.

 This book assumes that you have some basic knowledge of AWS, so we won't be diving into the basics of AWS IAM here. If you need a refresher on IAM, please visit the AWS documentation (*https:// oreil.ly/q4XYm*).

# The Principle of Least Privilege

"Can you give me the same permissions Roland has, so I can do my work faster?" We are 100% certain that you've either asked or been asked a question like this. Without context, this request sounds harmless, but Roland's account *could* include permissions to delete infrastructure, data, or both. Assigning users the appropriate permissions is not simple, and getting it right usually involves some trial and error.

The *principle of least privilege* states that any account—human or machine—should be given only the permissions its user needs to complete their job. Let's look at how this plays out in our case study. Currently, the Automatoonz environment is set up to grant wide-ranging permissions to all members of the development team. How did this happen? Well, the security team had initially locked down their permissions, but the development team asked the security team for broader permissions so as not to obstruct development work. The development team leads, Aisha and Dave, found themselves doing a great deal of back-and-forth with the security team. They eventually pressured the security team to grant wider permissions.

As Automatoonz grows, the compliance team lead, Lorena, has made it clear that this security arrangement is a problem. Unless it's changed, the company will not be certified to work in different geographies, nor will it comply with security frameworks such as NIST 800-53, an industry-agnostic security framework used globally by compliance teams to standardize their security capabilities. The NIST 800-53 standard mandates (*https://oreil.ly/X4eGM*) that organizations use (and provide verification that they use) the principle of least privilege. Not following this standard will deter partners and keep the company's customer base from growing.

To prove this point, Lorena cites numerous recent examples of incidents that put Automatoonz's business objectives at risk—incidents that resulted from these wider permissions. For instance, during the last quarter, the audit team and the development team were both granted superuser permissions on their AWS accounts. This meant they could remediate misconfigurations and develop products at their own speeds. The security team noticed that some of their AWS resources, like S3 and EBS volumes, were not encrypted, so they created a KMS encryption key and began encrypting these volumes. But since the security team did not know who was accessing data, or from where, they could not customize the KMS key policy to the appropriate roles. They simply locked access to the entire development team's storage. Lorena points out that if the security team only had the ability to *read* resource misconfigurations, it would not have been able to temporarily lock access to the development team's storage.

In another example from the current quarter, the finance team repeatedly warned the development team that their EC2 billing was over budget. To get the finance team off their backs, Dave and Aisha decided to delete some instances that they did not recognize, assuming they were old resources. In a couple of hours, it became clear that they had in fact deleted active resources being used by the art design team. Lorena points out that Dave and Aisha should not have had permissions to delete other teams' resources.

According to the compliance team, Automatoonz has only a loose definition of who has which permissions, and this situation is affecting the productivity of multiple teams.

First, let's be clear that these problems are not just IAM problems. IAM is one of many technical controls used to prevent mishaps like the ones Lorena noted. We need to evaluate the situation holistically, at 10,000 feet. We can do this using the People, Process, Technology triad for IAM security, as shown in Table 5-1.

*Table 5-1. Overall themes within the People, Process, Technology triad for IAM security*

| People | Process | Technology |
|---|---|---|
| Who is responsible for fixing problems? | How are tasks and responsibilities divided? | What AWS tools are used for prevention and detection? (E.g., GuardDuty, IAM Access Analyzer, service control policies, permission boundaries.) |
| Who is responsible for setting standards? | What is the escalation path? | What metrics are used to measure the health of these tools? |
| Which team is responsible for testing new preventive/corrective/detective controls? | How are exceptions handled? | Notify the responsible team through SNS. |

This is where the principle of least privilege comes into play. If users are being given permissions beyond the scope of what they need to do their jobs, you have a problem waiting to happen. Automatoonz has had two big incidents in just one year where people with excessive permissions inadvertently hindered the productivity of another team. Even though their intentions are not in question here, their actions adversely affected the entire company. Also, from an audit standpoint, the principle of least privilege is a must-have in most compliance frameworks, so not following it also creates negative repercussions for the company.

In our careers, we have seen entire production databases get deleted simply because someone had permissions to do so, and there was no second layer of defense or verification. In startups, when teams are still small, this usually happens because a few people are granted broad administrative permissions. The company then grows, but the permissions are never revoked or reassessed.

# Fine-Tuning Access Controls

We have seen people push back on having fine-grained access controls through IAM because the fine-tuning of IAM policies never ends. If you start a user with 10 permissions on day 1, they need 2 more on day 10 and 5 more on day 20. Fast-forward to day 365, and the user has been granted nearly all permissions because "they're needed." Where does it stop? And why put in all the effort to grant fine-grained user permissions if everyone is just going to end up with broad permissions?

First, you need to know that it *is* impossible to get access controls right in one shot. You will need to iterate to some extent. To reasonably include IAM controls in your DevSecOps plan, there are a few overarching strategies that we recommend building into your IAM automation pipeline. Let's go through these strategies and break them down one at a time.

## Use a Tagging System

The first component to build is a tagging system. AWS provides resource tagging as a governance feature: you can tag AWS resources, such as IAM policies and roles, or non-IAM resources, like EC2 instances, using a key/value pair. For example, if you want to identify an IAM role being used by the game development team, you might use a tag value of `team:gamedev`. In this example, `team` is the key, and `gamedev` is the value.

IAM and AWS resource tagging work well together. The benefits of using tagging include:

- Standardized resource naming for ease of understanding
- Data classification to identify sensitive resources
- Owner or team tags that show which teams own which resources
- Automation and/or security tags to prevent automated actions on certain resources

---

## A Story from the Trenches

One of the authors worked with a team that created an infrastructure that functioned as, at a very high level, a combination of information collector and resource deletor. The resource deletor cleaned up the environment every *x* days to prevent the

---

company's AWS account from accruing stale resources and racking up bills. After the first month of deployment, the team noticed that this infrastructure was not really helping to reduce costs; in fact, the AWS bill *increased* after they deployed it.

Upon investigation, the team found that the deletor component had deleted the collector component! This means that the collector couldn't carry out its job of querying resources for deletion, leading to undeleted resources.

If the deletor function had had the ability to identify resources by tag and was instructed not to delete resources tagged as core to the account's functioning, this situation could have been avoided. Not only is tagging important for identification, it also serves as an attribute for applying automation to specific resources.

Within AWS, resources allow access to certain permissions through tags and their respective values.

Let's look at an example permission policy that implements tagging:

```
{
    "Version": "2012-10-17",
    "Statement": [{
        "Effect": "Allow",
        "Action": "iam:DeleteUser",
        "Resource": "*",
        "Condition": {"StringEquals": {"iam:ResourceTag/type": "temp"}}
    }]
}
```

This policy allows deletion of IAM users who have the tagged key `type` and the value `temp`. The intent of the policy is to prevent accidental deletion of any other type of user by only allowing deletion of temporary users, such as external auditors, contractors, or interns.

## Clarify Team Responsibilities

It is difficult to build and/or validate IAM permissions for any user—human or machine—without understanding what that user needs to do. Each team has a set of responsibilities and must access certain resources as part of its operations. The earlier you understand what the teams will use for their jobs, the easier it will be for you to build appropriate IAM policies. Within Automatoonz, for example, the developer team is only responsible for spinning EC2 instances up or down if they own the instances. They should not be allowed to terminate or stop instances that do not belong to them.

The level of rigor and granularity in your IAM controls should increase as you get closer to your production environment. Similarly, the ratio of human identities to machine identities should substantially decrease as you get closer to production. Your automation (via machine identities) should be doing predictable, known deployments. Keep humans as far away from the production environment as possible to avoid human-induced errors.

Teams will often explore services as they learn about or build something new. For example, your developer team may have permissions to spin up SageMaker instances for learning or exploring, but not in production environments. Such checks can be implemented at the AWS Organizations level using service control policies (SCPs). SCPs are IAM-like JSON documents that allow or deny execution of AWS API calls over an AWS account or a group of AWS accounts (if you apply the SCPs onto an Organizational unit).

## Prevent and Detect

In Chapter 3, you learned about the importance of both prevention and detection in security. Staying true to course, we recommend implementing IAM controls at both the preventive and detective levels.

As a quick recap, *preventive controls* will block any misconfiguration before it happens in the AWS infrastructure. For example, if you tried to create a public S3 bucket, a preventive control might prohibit that action to prevent you from exposing your data.

*Detective controls* inform you of any misconfigurations in your AWS environment (after resources have been initiated/built). The AWS service GuardDuty is a good example of a detective control.

Together, these two types of controls complement each other. Detective controls can help you find out what your preventive controls do *not* cover, and how effective they are. Sticking to our previous example, if you add a preventive control to stop anyone from creating a public S3 bucket, you could use a detective control to check for public S3 buckets. If you find one, this indicates that your preventive control is not working correctly.

Detective controls that are *not* mapped to preventive controls are also a great feedback loop for preventive controls. If your detective controls find a surge of some particular violation in your environment, that could be a sign that you should invest in a preventive control to avoid that type of violation.

AWS provides many preventive and detective controls as services. Let's look at a few of them.

Preventive controls in AWS include:

*Service control policies (SCPs)*
    SCPs allow or deny specific APIs, which can be applied on an AWS account or group of AWS accounts.

*Permissions boundary*

> An additional layer of permission that prevents any IAM role from expanding its permissions beyond what is included in the permissions boundary.

Detective controls in AWS include:

*IAM Access Analyzer*

> This will tell you if your resources are accessing material, or being accessed, outside your zone of trust (i.e., outside your account or organization).

*GuardDuty*

> A machine learning–based threat detection service that alerts you when IAM access patterns deviate from a baseline.

*AWS Config rules*

> AWS Config is a service that tracks the state of AWS resources and their individual configurations. AWS Config rules allow you to take actions or set alerts for certain configuration changes to resources. These rules can be custom or managed by AWS. For example, if you want to check whether backup is enabled for a database you created, you could use a Config rule to detect that. AWS provides an ever-growing list of Config rules, which are listed in its documentation (*https://oreil.ly/A8oUW*).

# The IAM Pipeline

To implement the concepts you've just learned, let's return to Automatoonz, where the security team is getting requests to approve the developer team's IAM policies. In this section, you'll help them create a pipeline that can allow the developers to verify the sanity of their IAM policies themselves, or assist the security team in evaluating multiple IAM policies automatically, so they can get approvals out to the developer team as early as possible. The functionalities of the pipeline are dependent on who will use the pipeline.

> The architecture we are suggesting here is an extension of the pipeline we created in the earlier chapters. For simplicity, it uses just one open source tool. Feel free to modify and use it according to your needs.

The architecture diagram in Figure 5-1 shows the IAM pipeline we'll build. Let's say that Dave (developer team lead at Automatoonz) will first commit his IAM policies into the CodeCommit repository that houses all the IaC components. The event of committing these IAM policies will trigger the pipeline we are building here, which contains an open source IAM scanner. This scanner will provide feedback via build logs to tell Dave whether the IAM policies he just committed are secure. Typically, these kinds of tools are called *linters*. They will scan for issues in your code without actually executing it.

The dotted line in Figure 5-1 that runs from the security team to the CodeBuild project is meant to show that the IAM scanner in the pipeline is configured by a security team member, but is not part of the pipeline code.

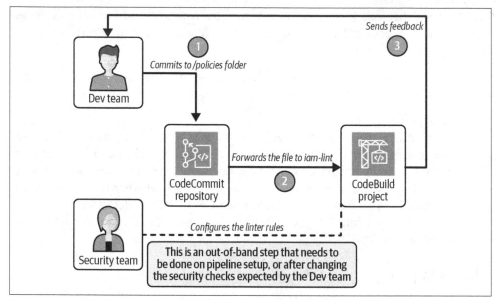

*Figure 5-1. High-level architecture for IAM linting*

To build the IAM pipeline, you'll first create a new directory in the Automatoonz repository you created in Chapter 2. To do that, go to the cloned repository in your system, and run the following command:

```
> mkdir iam-policies/
```

Create a new file inside this directory called *requested-iam.json*. This is the file Dave is asking the security team to evaluate. Copy and paste the following code into this file:

```
{
    "Version": "2012-10-17",
    "Statement": [
        {
            "Sid": "VisualEditor0",
            "Effect": "Allow",
            "Action": [
                "s3:DeleteObjectVersion",
                "s3:DeleteObject",
                "s3:DeleteBucket"
            ],
```

```
            "Resource": "*"
        }
    ]
}
```

Upload this new file to the Automatoonz repository using the git commit command.

Now, let's switch gears to the Automatoonz security team and figure out how they can scan insecure IAM files at scale. For this task, we'll be working with another popular open source tool known as Parliament (*https://oreil.ly/wASc2*) that helps identify possible security issues with IAM JSON files. In order to automate this scan, install Parliament in the CodeBuild project.

The modified build file will look like this:

```
version: 0.2

phases:
  install:
    commands:
      - echo Entering the install phase...
      - gem install cfn-nag
      - pip install parliament
  build:
    commands:
      - echo Entering the build phase...
      - cfn_nag_scan --input-path $CODEBUILD_SRC_DIR
      - parliament --directory $CODEBUILD_SRC_DIR/iam-policies
```

Once you've edited the build file on your local machine, commit it to the repository so that the new build file is updated for your CodePipeline. Once you push the commit, you'll see the CodePipeline start to run. If everything runs correctly, your CodeBuild logs should look like Figure 5-2.

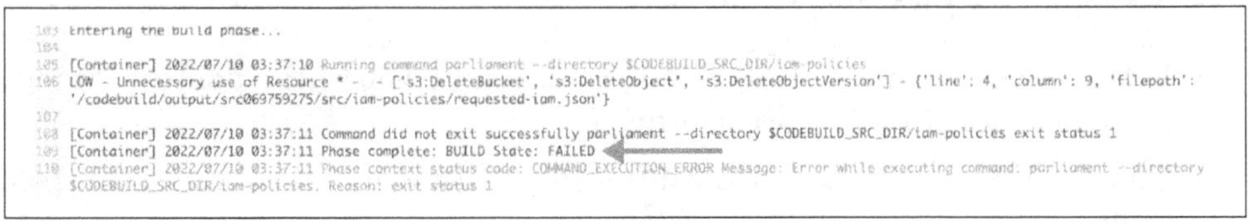

*Figure 5-2. Output of CodeBuild failure*

Let's look more closely at the code in Figure 5-2, specifically the line that starts with the word LOW:

```
LOW - Unnecessary use of Resource * --
['s3:DeleteBucket', 's3:DeleteObject', 's3:DeleteObjectVersion'] -
{'line':4, 'column':9, 'filepath':'/codebuild/output/src069759275/src/
iam-policies/requested-iam.json'}
```

This is a finding from the Parliament scanner, which says that the IAM policy you uploaded has an asterisk: *. This means it is applicable to all resources. As you know, the principle of least privilege holds that you should be providing permissions for only what each user needs—including resources.

The output states that the build failed because using * as the policy resource is too permissive for general usage. The preventive controls in place specify that this policy should therefore be rejected. To automate this process even further, you could create an SNS topic that sends this failure message back to the person who made the commit, quickening the turnaround time for the IAM policy validation.

In addition to open source tools like `iam-lint` and Parliament, AWS has also launched an API within IAM Access Analyzer that validates IAM policies for syntactical and security issues. You can make this API part of your CI/CD pipeline.

## Summary

This chapter introduced the principle of least privilege, which, as you learned, is important not just from a security perspective but from operational and compliance standpoints as well. You saw that implementing IAM controls in AWS is not a fixed, one-time task, but an evolving process that involves planning, execution, and iteration. You also now know why it's so important to understand a user's need for an IAM permission before provisioning the IAM policy for it.

We also revisited the topic of preventive and detective controls. You learned that they are equally important in understanding how well your IAM is implemented, and that tagging resources is an important first step in implementing attribute-based access control within AWS.

A quick recap of key takeaways from this chapter:

- IAM is difficult to get right in one shot. Refine your IAM policies through prevention and detection mechanisms.
- Utilize AWS's tag-based access-control mechanisms to better scale your IAM controls.
- Clearly delineate team responsibilities as you build and test IAM policies within your AWS environment.
- Your team should do some deep dives into the IAM roles you're provisioning, enumerating the permissions and identifying unused roles. In short, it's wise to occasionally clean up the cobwebs in your IAM infrastructure.

# CHAPTER 6

# Fault Injection Test

Finding solutions for outdated monolithic applications and architectures can be difficult. In response to these architectural patterns, the use of microservices has grown exponentially. *Microservice architectures* help solve the challenges of monolithic systems by creating a "suite of small services" that can be deployed independently, according to software development expert Martin Fowler (*https://oreil.ly/qyLnc*). The advantages of these small, independent services include faster isolation and detection of bugs, and making services across the business reusable and simpler to deploy.

Of course, distributed architectures bring new challenges, especially in securing all the possible distributed components. For adversaries, distributed architectures provide many entry points to destroy, disrupt, steal, and cause havoc. These systems require proper security testing to identify any vulnerabilities. Improper, or nonexistent, security controls and testing can lead to undetected, unpredictable, and unanticipated failures.

This chapter will outline different types of distributed systems, the importance of testing, the consequences of insufficient testing, and what types of tests should be done.

## Distributed Systems

There are two types of distributed systems:

*Soft real-time distributed systems*
> These systems continually produce or update results, but the response time is higher than that of hard real-time distributed systems. Missing a job deadline isn't considered a system failure, but a performance degradation. Examples of soft real-time systems include virtual reality, mobile communication, and multimedia systems.

*Hard real-time distributed systems*

These are critical systems. They are *restrictive*, meaning that missing a job deadline results in a system failure. An error will invoke a computation reset, not a reset to a previous checkpoint. Typically, the response time of a hard real-time system is measured in milliseconds and the size of the data for processing should be small to medium. Examples of hard real-time systems include credit card transaction systems, traffic control systems, and the autopilot systems used in rocket launches.

## Adaptive Security Controls

Distributed systems (both soft and hard) require security controls that can adapt to changes in the environment—these are called *adaptive security controls*. These controls can monitor and evaluate their environments and modify their behaviors accordingly. Adaptive security controls typically work in two major stages. In the first stage, prediction, the controls anticipate and assess risk, then recommend any baseline security changes that should be made to the distributed systems. In the second stage, the controls implement those baseline security recommendations along with any other needed security controls, then conduct a retrospective analysis.

A simple example of an adaptive security control is one that analyzes the risk associated with a user's profile, login, and behavior. This control would analyze unsuccessful login attempts, unsuccessful multifactor authentication (MFA) attempts, and the real-time context of the device (for instance, if anyone is attempting access from unknown devices).

Security controls need to adapt to ensure compliance in all workloads. Distributed systems' workloads tend to be ephemeral, which influences how security teams view them. Cloud native approaches to building also affect how security is viewed. For example, if scheduled security vulnerability scans aren't catching short-lived workloads, this can create the potential for security gaps.

Merging a DevOps and site reliability engineering (SRE) (*https://oreil.ly/bdoRU*) culture with security is an opportunity to build security into the early stages of the development life cycle. Typically, workload deployments focus on the services provided; in some cases, hardening the security controls comes later in the deployment cycle. The DevSecOps culture recommends addressing security early on, which may require shifting communications and collaboration with business stakeholders and development and security teams. When security controls align with detection and Chaos Engineering, discussed later in this chapter, you'll be in much better shape to discover threats, streamline the path to production, and automate responses before attacks can do significant damage.

## The True Cost of Downtime

Malfunctioning or failing applications or systems can have long-lasting negative consequences for a company's reputation and bottom line. Depending on what your system does, an outage could harm a customer's productivity, prevent your customers from purchasing items, or bring a halt to business transactions. The costs of downtime can even ripple across a whole nation's economy. For example, in 2022, Rogers Communications, which provides about a quarter of the network connectivity for the entire nation of Canada, went down for 19 hours. This caused millions of people to lose access to banking, transportation, television, wireless, and government services. Analysts interviewed by BNN Bloomberg (*https://oreil.ly/dvf2M*) estimated the overall cost of the outage at about Can\$142 million. Bloomberg reported that Rogers initially offered customers a credit for two days' worth of service, but increased that to five days in hopes of "restoring Canadians' confidence in us."

Rogers' CEO explained (*https://oreil.ly/QgokR*) that the outage was due to a network system failure caused by a maintenance update to the core network. Rogers could have benefited from deep packet inspection (DPI) testing, a network surveillance mechanism that looks at the origins of data packets to ensure whether they are valid, even delaying and prioritizing their delivery if needed. DPI testing helps manage congestion and can help engineers tweak their network architectures to avoid potential issues in the future. Such testing might well have uncovered the vulnerability in Rogers' network before it affected millions of customers.

As the example of the Rogers outage shows, downtime comes with high costs. Understanding the wider effects of outages has changed how engineering teams track the cost of downtime as a metric and a *key performance indicator* (KPI)—a common way to provide data points showing progression toward set goals.

# Methods for Minimizing Downtime

All organizations want to minimize the cost of downtime, but their approaches for *how* to do so vary widely. A few examples of methods for minimizing downtime include:

*Security as a service*
> Security as a service offloads the operational burden of managing the security-related infrastructure components, so teams can focus on identifying configurations for their security controls.

*Pay-as-you-consume*
> The pay-as-you-consume approach allows security controls to handle both short-lived and long-lived workloads. This helps to offset costs, since the organization doesn't have to pay for 24/7 security controls for workloads that only need 24-hour service 5 days a week.

*Lightweight agents*
Agents that provide bidirectional communications generally offer enriched security features like firewalls, intrusion prevention tools, and vulnerability scanning tools. Lightweight agents can help in correlating events and identifying incidents.

*Severity incident management*
Severity incident (SEV) management standardizes practices to better identify and focus on meaningful details of an incident, from a "blameless" mindset.

*Root cause analysis*
Root cause analysis (RCA) reports focus on learning how and why a problem occurred and finding supporting evidence for those reasons. Teams can use RCA reports to develop an action plan to prevent future incidents and outline next steps, such as updating the team's skill set or running a simulation.

*Simulations*
Running simulations of disruptive attacks can help identify issues that require architectural or workload modifications before they cause downtime. These are essentially "fire drills" to smooth out processes and identify weaknesses.

*Failure testing*
Failure testing is when certain environmental variables or scenarios are applied to systems or applications that produce a binary result. When the wrong outcome is produced, a failure will occur (an expected result).

*Fault injection*
Fault injection is a kind of security testing that aims to see how a service or application reacts to failures, but does not necessarily try to break it intentionally. You can use this method to prepare for unexpected or difficult-to-anticipate cascading impairments to or outages in your systems. Fault injection allows you to methodically walk through your systems or environments, placing failures, and replicate production incidents in a controlled manner.

Using, developing, and fine-tuning metrics that result from methods like those listed here can help summarize information about your system's efficiency, effectiveness, quality, timeliness, governance, compliance, behaviors, personnel performance, and resource utilization.

The rest of this chapter focuses on the benefits of testing via simulation. Specifically, we'll focus on Chaos Engineering.

# Chaos Engineering

Have you ever heard of the butterfly effect? In 1972, mathematician Edward Lorenz gave a speech to the American Association for the Advancement of Science about this concept. He titled it "Predictability: Does the Flap of a Butterfly's Wings in Brazil Set

Off a Tornado in Texas?" (*https://oreil.ly/Uwhzr*). The idea prompted mathematicians to study how a small change in one or more systems, as a result of random actions, can cause significant changes to trajectories in a later state. That idea is now called Chaos Theory (*https://oreil.ly/HomVs*).

Chaos Engineering builds on the idea of Chaos Theory, reasoning that a small, random change—like a networking impairment in one cloud native network segment or geolocation (availability zones/region)—could propagate across organizations or environments, eventually leading to downtime or other catastrophic results. *Chaos Engineering*, in the context of software development and architecture, refers to methodically planned experiments that seek to understand how highly complex, large-scale systems respond to pseudorandom real-world events. Teams perform these experiments, then observe and capture metrics across the environment to map out the system's behaviors from end to end.

The term Chaos Engineering was coined at Netflix, where teams created an open source testing project to aid their migration to AWS. In the manifesto (*https://oreil.ly/y8Y6w*) they later wrote to formalize the idea, they define Chaos Engineering as "the discipline of experimenting on a distributed system in order to build confidence in the system's capability to withstand turbulent conditions in production."

The open source project, called Chaos Monkey, was a novel way of testing (*https://oreil.ly/IAux4*) for resiliency, fault tolerance, and availability by randomly selecting resources to terminate in environments across the enterprise *every day*. Two former Netflix engineers involved in this process, Casey Rosenthal and Nora Jones, have since written a book on the topic, *Chaos Engineering* (O'Reilly). Rosenthal and Jones write:

> Forms of Chaos Engineering have implicitly existed in many other industries for a long time. Bringing experimentation to the forefront, particularly in the software practices within other industries, gives power to the practice. Calling these out and explicitly naming it Chaos Engineering allows us to strategize about its purpose and application, and take lessons learned from other fields and apply them to our own.

Netflix later introduced a collection of failure injection tools called the Simian Army (*https://oreil.ly/Mp06Q*). This toolset facilitated Chaos Engineering, allowing users to intentionally induce abnormalities and instructing engineers to respond accordingly. The goal of this testing practice is to be scientific about measuring results of the intentional injection from a stimulus, and to minimize the "blast radius" of affected resources.

## Basic Principles

The *Principles of Chaos Engineering* manifesto structures this approach according to the scientific method (*https://oreil.ly/TqKP0*). The four basic principles of Chaos Engineering, according to the manifesto, are:

1. Start by defining "steady state" as some measurable output of a system that indicates normal behavior.

2. Hypothesize that this steady state will continue in both the control group and the experimental group.

3. Introduce variables that reflect real-world events like servers that crash, hard drives that malfunction, network connections that are severed, etc.

4. Try to disprove the hypothesis by looking for a difference in steady state between the control group and the experimental group.

These principles, however, differ from the traditional scientific method. For instance, Chaos Engineering assumes that your control group is a stable system, whereas in the scientific method independent variances are introduced to the control group. Furthermore, to build confidence in the system's fault tolerance, Chaos Engineering introduces turbulence to the steady state.

This allows the engineers to concentrate on understanding the system, and not just focus on the root cause of a particular problem, shifting the mindset from tunnel vision to one of "trust but verify." This helps everyone to avoid getting too deep in the weeds, which is distracting from the task at hand.

In the rest of this section, we'll look at each of these four principles more deeply.

### Principle 1: Define your steady state

The first step in Chaos Engineering is to capture what a normal operational system looks like. Decide what metrics you want to observe. For example, if an application has just been deployed into an environment, you would start running load tests in increments: low, daily, peak, and projected-growth traffic times:

*Low traffic*
> Depending on your business model, low traffic times might be after 10:00 P.M. in a particular time zone, when most people are sleeping and there is less usage.

*Daily traffic*
> Daily traffic represents a normal business day. For instance, traffic could start at 9:30 A.M. in a particular time zone, because that's when a trading market opens.

*Peak traffic*
> Peak traffic is a time when most of your target audience is active, such as an annual holiday sales event.

*Projected-growth traffic*

Projected-growth traffic volume is a mix of historical data from the year before and what the business analysts predict for the coming year. For example, a lifestyle or fitness company might expect 100% growth in new subscriptions or memberships between November and February. These projections are normally generated by the developer and QA teams.

You can repurpose the metrics from the initial load test and form a baseline. Here are some basic metrics to get you started, but be sure to choose metrics that are meaningful for your organization's specific needs:

*Technical metrics*
- Health checks of endpoints
- Average CPU usage
- Memory usage
- Latency
- Storage availability
- Location impairment outage (geolocation or region)
- Malformed responses (improper syntax)

*Business metrics*
- Number of failed logins per minute during a high-traffic time frame
- Number of failed transactions per second
- Number of delayed responses within a threshold
- Scaling events

You should continuously refine the data further by incrementally monitoring and adjusting the threshold values of alerts and alarms. For example, using increments of 24 hours, 1 week, 1 month, 3 months, 6 months, 1 year, and 2 years is a good way to capture trends and inform operators of the quality and quantity of data being captured or logged. In this example, we might observe the following:

- In 24 hours, the information can be used to represent the current state of the environment.
- In 1 week, you have data that represents full cycles of low, daily, and peak traffic behaviors and patterns.
- In 1 month, you can begin weeding out data quality issues, such as reducing noise (which leads to cost savings on compute and storage) or exposing new APIs to meaningful metrics. The 3-month and 6-month increments offer similar benefits and allow for different patterns to emerge.

- In 1 year, you have a holistic view of your environment and supporting data for scaling and depreciation opportunities for the organization.
- You can use the 2-year baseline to validate trends and patterns seen in the 1-year data.

Baselines are the foundation of what a steady state really represents. The organization's goals and business models will change over time, and teams are expected to stay ahead of those changes.

### Principle 2: Build a hypothesis

Next, build a hypothesis around the steady state behavior you have defined. Will the steady state hold when you perform actions that are potentially harmful to network latency, applications, nodes, or other components of the system?

### Principle 3: Introduce real-world events as variables

This is where you will deploy destructive experiments to detect deviations. The idea here is to simulate (or replicate) real-world events that have happened or could happen to similar system designs. Develop experiments that simulates users' or applications' experiences. For instance:

- What happens if the service is not available?
- What happens if there is too much traffic, or bottlenecks in the network? How does that impact the service?
- What can go wrong while deploying new application features?
- If there are single points of failure, are there error notifications upon failure?
- What if a network failure causes high rates of "access denied" errors?

We provide a detailed example of such an experiment later in this chapter.

### Principle 4: Try to disprove your hypothesis

If any deviations have occurred after the destructive experiments were deployed, that will uncover an underlying weakness in the system. If the steady state does not change, the same experiments will validate whether the hypothesis holds.

## Advanced Principles

The authors of the *Principles of Chaos Engineering* manifesto also provide more advanced principles, which we'll quickly run through here; we recommend that you also read the manifesto in full.

## Run experiments in production

Building with confidence in staging is key to this principle. Typically, organizations experiment in staging environments after debugging and applying fixes. The stable changes are then promoted to production. Running an experiment in production is an advanced technique to uncover any hidden differences between staging and production that are unknown or not accounted for, to avoid causing impairment or damage.

## Automate experiments to run continuously

Automation gives you the ability to run experiments throughout your different environments using continuous delivery pipelines. For example, you might choose to schedule events to run on your systems in different increments, similar to cron jobs. This allows you to cover a large or growing set of experiments while reducing the risk of human error.

The exercise of having these experiments continuously running in the background gives you more time to focus on growth and scaling in the environment. You can use historical data to build reports around deployment failures related to permission or policy changes on IAM roles and networking. You can add metadata to resources to identify and notify the appropriate departments or teams to resolve potential issues before production. This new knowledge can help empower teams to identify or prevent technical debt for future modifications and systemic unknowns.

If you capture your automation experiments in code, you can empirically adjust your initial conclusions over time. This will extend to other systems outside of your immediate scope. Keep in mind that dependencies within systems can change to a large enough degree to create vulnerabilities. For example, if your system is tightly coupled and not modular in nature, changing an application's security policy can trigger a service impairment to a database. That change could even start a cascade of access issues for multiple applications in a completely different part of your environment if you've been reusing the same application security role. To take another example, a team could go into firefighting mode to fix an issue and decide to relax a security policy to stop the bleeding (the immediate service impairment). However, this could unintentionally introduce a new behavior or bug in the environment that is hidden from other teams in the system.

When using automation to track changes throughout a complex system, standardizing the way you manage new or existing modifications is the key to preventing unintended consequences. Clear conventions will help you train new members on your team and ensure everyone understands the upstream and downstream flows to different endpoints and the volume of the traffic in the environments. By keeping communication open and making the learning curve minimal, you prevent technical debt that would negatively impact your organization.

### Minimize the blast radius

When deploying, you can reduce the risk to production environments by using a *canary deployment* model. With this strategy, you roll out changes to a small subset of users (perhaps 2%) to start. As confidence grows, you begin rolling the changes out in phases to a larger subset of users: 5%, then 10%, 25%, 50%, 75%, and finally 100%. This incremental approach allows for fine-grained control, with the understanding that there may be some short-term service impact during this exercise.

You can exclude any high-value transactions from experiments that will impact the business if performed in production. Traffic mirroring is a technique you can apply to your network, replicating backend traffic to an endpoint and ignoring the application's responses. If an experiment fails, this will test the application's retry logic, monitor performance, and check for errors in logs.

It's important to understand that Chaos Engineering is a methodical framework for DevSecOps engineers to use as a guideline. Depending on your team's or organization's skill sets and maturity, you can and should tailor each principle to meet your specific needs.

## Chaos Engineering in AWS Environments

You can prepare for complex situations by adjusting or updating monitoring and alerting tools, operational runbooks, and disaster recovery drills. AWS Fault Injection Simulator (FIS) (*https://oreil.ly/kYPNL*) is a managed service that performs fault injection experiments on your environments in a controlled and methodical manner. The results of these experiments can be used to tune the performance and design of your applications. The experiments are captured in configuration files.

These disruptive simulations might include opening or closing ports on the network to observe how the systems or applications respond. You might restrict or relax user privileges or alter the access levels of IAM roles to observe weaknesses in the different defense layers.

With the new knowledge you gain by proving or disproving your assumptions, you can develop and implement new solutions in code. You can also educate the security team and the larger organization, transferring the knowledge. This deeper understanding can help everyone reduce technical debt.

As you run these experiments, you can invoke events in sequence or in parallel. You can control a sequence of actions to cause gradual degradation in the environment. For example, you might intermittently increase latency, then increase storage consumption, and then trigger the escalation or removal of IAM privileges or policies. Figure 6-1 is a high-level diagram of such a workflow. The AWS FIS templates are located in the book's GitHub repository (*https://oreil.ly/SaCgh*).

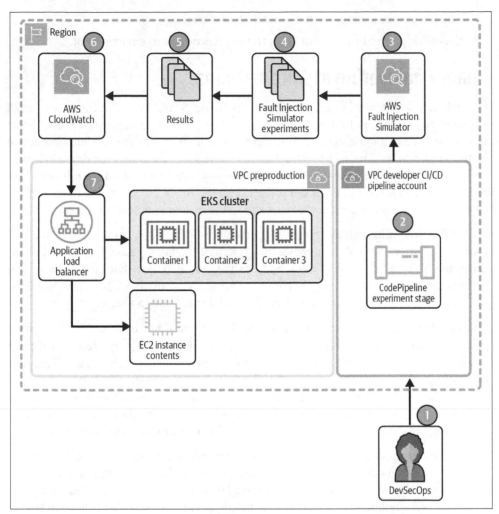

*Figure 6-1. Integrating AWS FIS experiments with an existing CI/CD pipeline*

The workflow shown in Figure 6-1 is as follows:

1. The DevSecOps engineer adds a chaos experiment stage to an existing CI/CD pipeline to run FIS tests.
2. The DevSecOps engineer adds additional commands to have the CI/CD pipeline invoke the AWS FIS APIs.
3. The DevSecOps engineer sets up the proper IAM roles and access, with approval from leadership, to use the AWS FIS managed service.
4. The FIS managed service processes the FIS experiment templates.
5. After the simulation runs, the results from the FIS templates are output.

6. The FIS results are logged in CloudWatch for tracking.

7. EventBridge event rules route back to the preproduction environment.

# Chaos Engineering at Automatoonz

Our friends at Automatoonz are facing a new issue. Scott, from the inventory management team, notices that he hasn't received any new logs since last week. Scott *should* be receiving log entries at 5-minute intervals from a heartbeat function active in the applications. The fact that he hasn't received any new logs for days definitely seems odd, since he's heard in standup meetings that Bex, Aisha, and Dave are building on AWS. Scott reaches out to Bex, who confirms that the game development team has been deploying infrastructure and has launched two new instances.

Scott, alarmed, calls an emergency meeting with DevSecOps lead Ravi to find the root cause. After hours of debugging, they find that the log ingestion service has been dropping all logs for the past week because the load balancer that's fronting the log storage system has not been connected to anything. Automatoonz has effectively lost a whole week's worth of logs—and it took a week for anyone to notice.

You can have all the logging in the world, but if you don't have disk space, you'll get errors during stream ingestion, like `IOError:[Errno 28] No space left on device close failed in file object destructor:<file_path>`. This, Ravi tells his colleague, essentially creates a "black hole" in the network. The load balancer doesn't know it isn't connected; unaware of any issues with the active node, it simply continues to send ingress and egress requests, then drops them silently, without informing the destination. This creates gaps in the team's monitoring system.

Ravi proposes making Chaos Engineering experiments a priority for the DevSecOps team, to help them develop the proper configurations of logs, alarms, and alerts that will prevent similar incidents in the future. He wants to work with Bex and Dave to build a self-healing system, ensuring that their application is built to reconstruct itself with minimal downtime. They can confirm that it works by running test cases in which part of a system, or even an entire system, goes offline.

# AWS Fault Injection Simulator Experiment Examples

Using FIS can help you uncover security issues. This section provides some FIS examples to give you a starting point for your own experiments. The FIS experiment templates provided here are in JSON format and can be created using the following AWS CLI command:

```
> aws fis create-experiment-template \
    --cli-input-json file://template-configuration-file.json \
    --query experimentTemplate.id
```

The output after running the command should look like the following:

XXTQGyuiD7CZqWH1

# Kubernetes Pod Stress Testing

This first FIS template is used to stress test the CPU for Kubernetes pods for 5 minutes. This experiment helps to identify security compromises that could overwork the Kubernetes pods. The template looks like this:

```
{
    "description": "EKS ChaosMesh StressChaos example",
    "targets": {
        "EKS-Cluster-Target-1": {
            "resourceType": "aws:eks:cluster",
            "resourceArns": [
                "arn:aws:eks:arn:aws::111122223333:cluster/cluster-id"
            ],
            "selectionMode": "ALL"
        }
    },
    "actions": {
        "TestCPUStress": {
            "actionId": "aws:eks:inject-kubernetes-custom-resource",
            "parameters": {
                "maxDuration": "PT2M",
                "kubernetesApiVersion": "chaos-mesh.org/v1alpha1",
                "kubernetesKind": "StressChaos",
                "kubernetesNamespace": "default",
                "kubernetesSpec":
"{\"selector\":{\"namespaces\":[\"default\"],\"labelSelectors\":
    {\"run\":\"nginx\"}},\"mode\":\"all\",\"stressors\":
{\"cpu\":{\"workers\":1,\"load\":50}},\"duration\":\"5m\"}"
            },
            "targets": {
                "Cluster": "EKS-Cluster-Target-1"
            }
        }
    },
    "stopConditions": [{
        "source": "none"
    }],
    "roleArn": "arn:aws:iam::111122223333:role/role-name",
    "tags": {}
}
```

The output after running the command should look like the following:

EXTQGyuiHu8ZqYU1

## Throttling EC2 API Calls

In this next example, a FIS template is used to throttle 100% of the EC2 API calls for 10 minutes using a specific IAM role. This experiment helps to identify a potentially compromised IAM role. Here's the template:

```
{
  "tags": {
    "Name": "IAMThrottleEC2APIActions"
  },
  "description": "Throttle the EC2 APIs using a specified IAM role",
  "targets": {
    "myRole": {
      "resourceType": "aws:iam:role",
      "resourceArns": ["arn:aws:iam::111122223333:role/role-name"],
      "selectionMode": "ALL"
    }
  },
  "actions": {
    "ThrottleAPI": {
      "actionId": "aws:fis:inject-api-throttle-error",
      "description": "Throttle APIs for 10 minutes",
      "parameters": {
        "service": "ec2",
        "operations":
            "DescribeInstances,DescribeNetworkInterfaces,DescribeVolumes",
        "percentage": "100",
        "duration": "PT10M"
      },
      "targets": {
        "Roles": "myRole"
      }
    }
  },
  "stopConditions": [
    {
      "source": "aws:cloudwatch:alarm",
      "value":
      "arn:aws:cloudwatch:us-east-1:111122223333:alarm:alarm-name"
    }
  ],
  "roleArn": "arn:aws:iam::111122223333:role/role-name"
}
```

The output after running the command should look like the following:

```
XXPQGyuiHo9ZqWV6
```

It's important to remember to use the absolute path to the FIS configuration files to avoid relative path errors.

## Stress Testing the CPU on an EC2 Instance

In this example, a FIS template is used to stress test the CPU on an EC2 instance for 2 minutes using a predefined AWS Systems Manager (SSM) document called *AWSFIS-Run-CPU-Stress*.

The SSM document is configured to run the CPU stress test on an EC2 instance using the `stress-ng` tool. If `stress-ng` is not already installed on the EC2 instance, this SSM document will install it.

Going through the process of stressing the CPU is informative and will give you an edge in dealing with operating system vulnerabilities like Meltdown and Spectre. Meltdown, as Graz University of Technology researchers write (*https://oreil.ly/K5fMF*), "allows a program to access the memory, and thus also the secrets, of other programs and the operating system."

Here is the FIS template to stress test the CPU:

```
{
  "tags": {
      "Name": "EC2CPUStress"
  },
  "description": "Run a CPU fault injection on a specific EC2 instance",
  "targets": {
      "myInstance": {
          "resourceType": "aws:ec2:instance",
          "resourceArns": ["arn:aws:ec2:us-east-1:111122223333:instance/
            instance-id"],
          "selectionMode": "ALL"
      }
  },
  "actions": {
      "CPUStress": {
          "actionId": "aws:ssm:send-command",
          "description": "Run CPU stress test on EC2 using SSM",
          "parameters": {
              "duration": "PT5M",
              "documentArn": "arn:aws:ssm:us-east-1::document/
                AWSFIS-Run-CPU-Stress",
              "documentParameters": "{\"DurationSeconds\": \"120\",
                \"InstallDependencies\": \"True\", \"CPU\": \"0\"}"
          },
          "targets": {
              "Instances": "myInstance"
          }
```

```
        }
    },
    "stopConditions": [
        {
            "source": "aws:cloudwatch:alarm",
            "value": "arn:aws:cloudwatch:us-east-1:111122223333:alarm:alarm-name"
        }
    ],
    "roleArn": "arn:aws:iam::111122223333:role/role-name"
}
```

 It's critical to check for CVE updates and routinely update the environment's firmware, software, and applications (such as BIOS and OS) to prevent unauthorized access from attackers.

## Terminating an EC2 Instance

In this example, an FIS template is used to terminate an EC2 instance using a predefined SSM document called *AWS-TerminateEC2Instance*. The `maxDuration`, specifying the time allocated for this task to complete, is set to 5 minutes. The prerequisite is that the SSM agent is already installed on the EC2 instance.

This experiment helps to identify behaviors that could indicate a security compromise, such as a Denial of Service attack or an attacker gaining unauthorized access.

If you have autoscaling set up properly, you should expect to see another EC2 instance spin up to replace the one that was terminated within a few minutes. If you've set up monitoring and alerting, members of your team should receive a notification that the EC2 instance has been terminated. The DevSecOps, operations, and development teams should check for descriptive error messages from the applications running on the terminated instances. If the logging is noisy and full of meaningless information, work with the development team to reduce the toil.

Here's the template:

```
{
    "description": "Terminate an EC2 Instance",
    "stopConditions": [
        {
            "source": "none"
        }
    ],
    "targets": {
    },
    "actions": {
        "terminateInstances": {
            "actionId": "aws:ssm:start-automation-execution",
```

```
            "description": "Terminate an EC2 Instance",
            "parameters": {
                "documentArn":
                    "arn:aws:ssm:us-east-1::document/AWS-TerminateEC2Instance",
                "documentParameters":
                    "{\"InstanceId\": \"EC2_INSTANCE_ID\",
                    \"AutomationAssumeRole\": \"SSM_ROLE_ARN\"}",
                "maxDuration": "PT5M"
            },
            "targets": {
            }
        }
    },
    "roleArn": "SSM_ROLE_ARN"
}
```

Taking an EC2 instance down is an exercise that should be performed daily to instill confidence across teams and organizations. It's a realistic fire drill that brings gaps in security, networking, and application design into focus.

## Removing Ingress and Egress Rules from a Security Group

In this example, a FIS template is used to remove ingress and egress rules from a security group using a predefined SSM document called *AWS-CloseSecurityGroup*. The prerequisite is that the SSM agent is already installed on the EC2 instance.

This experiment helps to identify security compromises that may occur as a result of eliminating ingress and egress traffic through a security group for AWS resources (depending on that traffic's access).

Security issues commonly stem from internal members not understanding the different components of the environment. They might remove access accidentally, not realizing that a rule was providing connectivity to a critical resource.

Here is the FIS template:

```
{
    "description": "Remove ingress and egress traffic rules for a given security
        group",
    "stopConditions": [
        {
            "source": "none"
        }
    ],
    "targets": {
    },
    "actions": {
        "terminateInstances": {
            "actionId": "aws:ssm:start-automation-execution",
            "description": "Remove ingress and egress traffic rules for a given
                AWS security group",
```

```
            "parameters": {
                "documentArn": "arn:aws:ssm:us-east-1::document/
                    AWS-CloseSecurityGroup",
                "documentParameters": "{\"SecurityGroupId\":
                    \"SECURITY_GROUP_ID\", \"AutomationAssumeRole\":
                    \"SSM_ROLE_ARN\"}",
                "maxDuration": "PT5M"
            },
            "targets": {
            }
        }
    },
    "roleArn": "SSM_ROLE_ARN"
}
```

Proper networking policies and routing are critical for services and applications to function as intended. Security group configurations and the resources they are attached to can change over time, with new features or changes in security policies, so it's important to keep up.

## Detaching an EBS Volume from an EC2 Instance

In this example, a FIS template is used to detach a crucial EBS volume from an EC2 instance using a predefined SSM document called *AWS-DetachEBSVolume*. The prerequisite is that the SSM agent is already installed on the EC2 instance.

This experiment can help detect scenarios in which an attacker could disassociate an EBS volume from an EC2 instance on the drive that stores sensitive data or passwords. If the attacker can reattach the EBS volume to an instance on which they have escalated privileges, they can steal data or gain access to other resources using the data obtained. Monitoring, alerts, and logging should inform the teams when there is a change in the resource's configuration, outside of a maintenance or deployment window. There should also be automation scripts to remove unused or abandoned EBS volumes.

Let's look at the FIS template:

```
{
    "description": "Detach an EBS Volume",
    "stopConditions": [
        {
            "source": "none"
        }
    ],
    "targets": {
    },
    "actions": {
        "terminateInstances": {
            "actionId": "aws:ssm:start-automation-execution",
            "description": "Detach an EBS Volume",
```

```
            "parameters": {
                "documentArn": "arn:aws:ssm:us-east-1::document/
                    AWS-DetachEBSVolume",
                "documentParameters": "{\"VolumeId\": \"EBS_VOLUME_ID\",
                    \"AutomationAssumeRole\": \"SSM_ROLE_ARN\"}",
                "maxDuration": "PT5M"
            },
            "targets": {
            }
        }
    },
    "roleArn": "SSM_ROLE_ARN"
}
```

Enforcing proper resource hygiene (such as ensuring that unused volumes are removed from the account) is important to prevent unintended data compromises and to reduce the cost of zombie EBS volumes.

# Summary

At the end of the day, testing is a tool that DevSecOps engineers can use to discover, explore, and verify environments. Chaos Engineering and FIS can help ensure that you have an automated process in place to prepare for (and react to) real-world or game day events. With the FIS experiments/templates in IaC, you can run fire drills and isolate potential issues before moving into a production environment.

A quick recap of key takeaways from this chapter:

- Monolithic and microservice architectures each have their pros and cons, and all teams must communicate openly to understand where vulnerabilities can present themselves.

- Educating yourself on methods for minimizing downtime is critical to the organization.

- Chaos Engineering is a framework for methodically uncovering unknown vulnerabilities and allowing you to better understand the strength of your system. This puts you in a position where you are not just putting out fires, but rather arming yourself with historical knowledge from real-life incidents.

# CHAPTER 7

# People and Processes

Up until this chapter, we have focused on technology. We've discussed how different types of tools help us achieve different security functions. But, just like every sound security program, we have to address the entirety of the People, Process, Technology framework, which we briefly introduced in Chapter 5. This framework was popularized in the 1990s (*https://oreil.ly/jwPQR*) by cryptography expert Bruce Schneier, who argues that these three things form the foundation of security. Security cannot be implemented with technology alone, nor can it be implemented with just people or just a process. Balancing the three lets us security-minded folks focus on building secure systems instead of spending 99% of our time responding to events.

Now that you know what security tools and setups you need to get your technology to a minimum viable state, this chapter will cover the people and processes related to securing your IaC. Before we dive in, we want to make it very clear that there is no one right way to manage people or processes related to securing your infrastructure. Each organization has its own approach, based on its size, culture, and team structure. The pointers we give in this chapter are derived from our personal experiences, and from common themes we have seen among organizations that have implemented DevSecOps successfully.

## People: Team Structures and Roles

In this chapter, we will refer to a DevSecOps "team," whose members are focused on this journey. There are certain high-level roles that an ideal DevSecOps team should have. In this context, a *role* does not necessarily mean one or two people; depending on the budget and the employees available, you can assign a single person or multiple people to carry out a role's responsibilities, or assign multiple roles to one person. In this section, we discuss roles related to security, development, compliance, and product management.

## Security Engineers

There are multiple subdisciplines in security: application security, cryptography, and network security, to name a few. In a DevSecOps context, you might want a security generalist. The fundamental concepts of security should be clear to your candidates, of course; if they don't know the basics of security, they won't be able to guide others. If the person is a specialist who has worked in container security extensively, that's a bonus! But, such expertise isn't a necessity. AWS provides guidance on security through its public documentation (*https://oreil.ly/9RQgG*). AWS also updates and launches features and services at breakneck speed. It is difficult to keep up with the pace, much less be proficient in all of the offerings. So, it is not mandatory that your security team be composed of experts in each and every AWS service from day one (and if you required that, you would have a very difficult time finding candidates). You want your security team to be aware of AWS services and features, generally, and familiar with the relevant security services.

One way to provide measurable milestones for your security team's proficiency is to help them earn the AWS security certification (*https://oreil.ly/vnqsQ*). AWS security is no different than other security concepts, but being comfortable with AWS security tools, specifically, may help alleviate any concerns and allow your security team to focus on what is most important in their jobs.

## Developers

In order to automate, maintain, and debug your DevOps toolchain, you need to have developers on your team. Remember, DevSecOps is not a fixed destination; you'll always be building, improving, and refining your approach. There is no single codebase you can clone to implement DevSecOps perfectly. For some organizations, a developer-heavy DevSecOps team is sufficient, while others do well with a team of security experts who know how to code. The important thing is that the lead developer role for your DevSecOps initiative should *not* be assigned to a part-timer.

We have seen organizations assign developers to DevSecOps initiatives on a one-off basis (which you should *not* do). In this framework, the developers build the DevSecOps toolchain and then go back to their primary team functions. This structure has two major issues. First, the organization spends time and resources building something it won't use long term, wasting resources. Second, the organization never actually ends up using DevSecOps consistently, which gives it a false sense of security. Over time, if no one is maintaining and updating the toolchain and security checks the developers built, then they will be abandoned. Your tooling must be constantly calibrated to align with changes in how your environment uses IaC, or it will fail or be discontinued.

Saying "I need a developer" is a very broad statement. Based on our experience, most DevSecOps teams include people who are familiar with (in no particular order):

*Coding languages*
> If you work in the tech industry, you know there is no dearth of coding languages out there. As a rule of thumb, those on your development team should have knowledge of at least one of the languages supported by an AWS SDK. We recommend Python and Go for AWS DevSecOps roles. You can find more details about supported languages in the documentation (*https://oreil.ly/7lXUz*).

*IaC tools*
> As you build infrastructure and automations within AWS, there is a very high possibility that you will need to use AWS CloudFormation, Terraform, or AWS Cloud Development Kit (CDK). We have also seen some organizations lend their own flavor to these tools—for example, creating wrappers around Terraform to customize the way their developers use it. A DevSecOps engineer should be familiar with at least one IaC tool to be able to build infrastructure within AWS.

*AWS*
> For members of your development team, we recommend one year or more of hands-on experience and/or one associate-level AWS certification. We are deep believers in Anton Chekhov's adage that "knowledge is of no value unless you put it into practice." We highly recommend prioritizing practical knowledge over theoretical knowledge. A developer who understands the sharp edges of implementing something on AWS will provide an invaluable point of view while building your DevSecOps practice.

*Version control systems (VCSs)*
> This is as simple as it gets: if you're writing code, you need some way to manage versioning and storage of that code. The two most common versioning systems are Git and Mercurial. We don't prefer one over the other, but having hands-on experience with a VCS helps developers to ramp up quickly.

*Shell scripting*
> You'll need to use some level of shell scripting to patch together the open source tooling used within your infrastructure (much like the infrastructure we've presented in this book). Being able to read and write at least basic bash scripts is also highly helpful in the realm of DevSecOps.

By no means is this a definitive list of every DevSecOps engineering skill. Depending on your organization, your team may need to ramp up additional skills and tools.

## Compliance Team

As you build secure infrastructures, it is imperative to keep track of the compliance status and operational health of your system. You might be thinking, "Why should compliance be part of a DevSecOps initiative? Compliance is all about audits and reporting."

Hear us out: in our experience, too often, the DevSecOps team only engages the compliance team when there is an escalation or an audit is about to happen. This last-minute inclusion sometimes leads to a scramble to provide data in time. However, when a few compliance team members help the DevSecOps engineers decide up front what data should be collected, things tend to operate much more smoothly. Engineers/developers can also help build reporting capabilities that feed data directly to the compliance team. This significantly reduces confusion when audits occur.

In fact, one of the most successful teams we've worked with built their reporting dashboards according to their compliance team's specifications. Engineers mainly used a tactical dashboard, while the compliance team had a "risk posture" dashboard that showed a 10,000-foot view of all the checks and balances. Your compliance team should be provided with data gathered from all the checks and balances in a normalized (or cleaned) and timely manner, so they have up-to-date information about the security posture of the organization.

It's crucial to include the compliance team in the DevSecOps journey early on. This helps ensure that your hard work scales to multiple teams, and that the business gets a solid return on investment.

## Product Manager

Not every security team has an engineering manager or a technical product manager. The title is not as important as the function here. We suggest defining this role as a person who looks at the DevSecOps initiative as a whole and represents the DevSecOps team at a strategic level.

A team of engineers that works in isolation without strategic alignment with the wider DevSecOps initiative will eventually be overlooked. They might not even be seen as contributing to the company's overall objectives. This is exactly where the "product manager" role fits in. Some of the responsibilities of this role include managing workflows, ensuring the engineers on the team are not overloaded with multiple requests, and acting as a "load balancer" for requests and work priorities. This role should also help the DevSecOps team align with the strategic goals of the organization, focusing on the team's objectives and improving morale.

## Team Structure

Throughout this book, we have followed Automatoonz as they secure IaC at scale with their existing teams and technologies. You've seen that Automatoonz is structured as siloed teams with individual team goals. These goals are not communicated with other teams, which has led to business disruptions.

If we were to draw the Automatoonz DevSecOps operating model, it would look something like Figure 7-1.

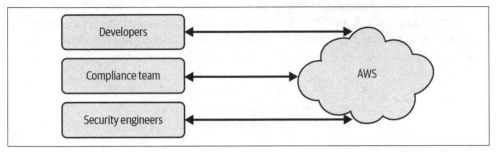

*Figure 7-1. Siloed operations at Automatoonz*

Everyone has direct access to the AWS cloud infrastructure, and everyone has their own methods of using the cloud. The lack of consistency and standardization is a result of the company's "do what works best for you" approach.

In a mature organization that has transitioned operations to the cloud and has been built around the skills and responsibilities mentioned in this section, these siloes are united. This unification is due to the common goals, practices, and processes engendered by DevSecOps principles. These principles include standardizing the procedures for making changes in the infrastructure. In short, if anyone needs to access (or change) the cloud infrastructure, there are certain rules they must follow. This more focused structure, based on DevSecOps principles, is shown in Figure 7-2.

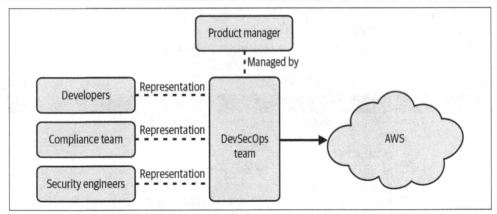

*Figure 7-2. Focused operations using DevSecOps*

Now that we've explored the people involved in securing IaC, let's move on to exploring the processes—how teams operate within this focused structure.

# Processes: Practices and Communication

As with the previous section, we want to remind you that the processes we discuss in this section are not a definitive list. Instead, we provide some guiding principles that you can implement as appropriate, depending on your organization's size and existing practices.

 Regardless of which practices you are following, we highly recommend having measurable goals and using metrics to determine the effectiveness of your processes. Defining and setting metrics is a science of its own; we will not go into detail in this chapter. If you're interested in learning more, we recommend *How to Measure Anything*, 3rd edition, by Douglas W. Hubbard (Wiley) and *How to Measure Anything in Cybersecurity Risk* by Douglas W. Hubbard et al. (Wiley).

## Communicate to the Right People, Consistently

As soon as you begin to implement any kind of change in an organization, you need to notify stakeholders at all levels, from leadership to the tactical workforce. Explain what the change brings to the organization and what resources it is going to require, and keep the stakeholders informed on your progress.

During this process, we've often seen people focus so hard on the good news that they end up not communicating the bad news. That is a big mistake. If you keep the blockers and hindrances hidden, your stakeholders will never know how to help you out. Be transparent and honest about what is working and what isn't. Table 7-1 outlines the basic building blocks of a typical status report.

*Table 7-1. Sample status report structure*

| Section | Includes | Example |
|---|---|---|
| Highlights | Things your team has successfully accomplished | We implemented IAM checks for 60% of projects in our environment. |
| Lowlights | Things your team could not implement successfully | Our team is being asked to remediate security misconfigurations, which is taking 40% of our time. |
| Trends | Metrics that show how your highlights and lowlights are trending | After implementing an IAM scanner upon submission, we saw a 15% uptick in detected security misconfigurations. |
| Upcoming objectives | Focus areas for the next cycle | We plan to ensure that all containers running in our environment have logging enabled and cannot be tampered with. |
| Blockers | Items currently at a standstill, and potentially a root cause for the issue | We have not been able to identify an SME for containers. |

Providing these high-level details helps you clearly and succinctly communicate to stakeholders what you have been working on and how it has been helping the organization. It also opens doors for people outside the team to contribute or guide the team through its blockers.

## Make Product Owners Accountable for Their Security Findings

If we could correct just one wrongheaded notion in organizations everywhere, it would be this one: "It's a security problem, so security should fix it."

We disagree with this school of thought. Security teams augment and assist the business objectives by making sure things are run securely, but the institutional knowledge of *why* something is built the way it is belongs to the relevant teams. For instance, when the members of a development team start building a particular feature, they go through the design process, weigh the risks and rewards, make decisions, and then build it. No one can explain that feature or provide background knowledge better than the development team that built it. So, when the security team detects a vulnerability with that feature, the team best equipped to address it is actually *development*. The security team can provide a second pair of eyes for verification or assistance in implementing a solution, but if the security team is pulled into remediating every misconfiguration that's found, it will never be able to keep up on its own. We've seen many security teams get overwhelmed this way, especially in large enterprises.

Every product team should be open to working with the security team to fix its misconfigurations, rather than just offloading the remediation. At the same time, if the security team notices a pattern of similar problems being repeated elsewhere in the organization, it should invest time in finding and fixing the root cause. If a new preventive or corrective control would solve the problem at a larger scale, security should take the lead in implementing it.

## Build Threat Modeling into Your Processes

If you aren't accustomed to including threat modeling in your processes, it can definitely feel like additional overhead. Yes, it is an extra step—but building threat models tells you whether your controls are covering those attack paths with the most potential to impact your workload.

Each time you build a threat model, some of the security vulnerabilities will have a constant security control associated with them. That is totally OK; in fact, this is how you will build your *control matrix*, a sort of library of your controls mapped to threats. Larger organizations usually track this control matrix using governance tools, such as RSA Archer. Smaller organizations often store it in accessible places such as wikis. Regardless of where your control matrix is stored, it should be updated regularly.

A great way to start creating your control matrix is to follow the Cloud Security Alliance's Cloud Control Matrix (CCM) (*https://oreil.ly/2cKxo*) model. At the time of writing, the CCM has close to 200 controls, spread across 17 security domains, which provide guidance on what security controls should be implemented in a cloud infrastructure. It also includes a security questionnaire designed to function as a starting point for the compliance team. To summarize: Start with CCM as your list of must-have controls in any application you build, then use a threat model to find any controls you should add or remove.

 Following the CCM model does *not* mean you can forget about threat modeling. The CCM is meant to be industry-agnostic, so it does not cover everything. Its controls are objective in nature, whereas you will need to make subjective calls about how to secure certain parts of your application. Something that poses a threat to *your* system might not be a threat for someone else. If you decide to use the CCM as a checklist, you *will* be bound to it. We recommend using CCM as a baseline, then employing threat modeling to find gaps in your security posture.

Let's look at an example to illustrate this idea. Suppose that you, much like our friends at Automatoonz, have an application that is externally exposed. Your users need to log in to use this application. Per the STRIDE model, which we discussed in Chapter 3, if MFA is enabled for your users, no malicious actor can spoof an authentic user's account. If you started off with the CCM, you already have a control matrix that includes a control statement for MFA. So, next time, if you see another application that has external users logging in, you'll know that you can address spoofing and repudiation concerns with your existing MFA pattern.

Now let's say that, in the same application, you need to authenticate your backend services using mutual Transport Layer Security (mTLS). This particular control is not present in the CCM, but mTLS is a security control, so you can add it to your control matrix for future use. Your final control matrix should contain references to all security controls that are present, missing, or need to be worked on for the application to be deployed.

Try to standardize the CCM controls where possible, whether they are detective, corrective, or preventive controls. We've seen threat models provide value by means of a secure pattern-generation tool. Let's look at an example from Automatoonz.

A few years ago, Lupe, who handles threat modeling for the Automatoonz security team, was asked to threat model four separate applications, all of which used SSH for their functionality. Every single one of these applications had the same need, but Lupe and the security team had to guide different teams on the same thing four separate times. Rather than keep this up, the security team decided to build a standardized secure SSH pattern, since that was the common denominator among all of these SSH use cases.

The next time a team came to Lupe for help with implementation of SSH, she simply provided the approved pattern and its associated requirements. Now, if the application meets the requirements, everyone can rest assured that it's using a secure, approved pattern, which accelerates the security team's review. The team can still consult with application owners if they have trouble meeting the requirements or if there's some special need not addressed by the pattern, but they are no longer wasting time and energy doing the same work multiple times.

## Build Roadmaps to Reach Your DevSecOps Goals

When building new initiatives, it is imperative to set SMART (specific, measurable, attainable, relevant, time-bound) goals for your team, on a quarterly basis at minimum. These team goals should, of course, align with your business's overall goals as well.

Here are some examples of next quarter's SMART goals for our friends at Automatoonz:

- As a security engineer, I should be able to identify AWS resources within our AWS accounts. (Scott, Inventory and Asset Management)
- As a compliance officer, I should be able to see the compliance coverage for our AWS workloads. (Lorena, Audit and Compliance)
- As a product manager, I should be able to identify the top security use cases and prioritize workloads for the DevSecOps team. (Bex, Product Manager, Security)

# What Next?

You are now at a pivotal stage, ready to take what you've learned in this book and implement it in your own workplace. If you are working in a corporate setting and the problems that Automatoonz is facing sound familiar, your workplace is likely a good candidate to adopt DevSecOps.

We know that adopting DevSecOps is easier said than done, however. As a first step, we urge you to list the use cases where security-focused automation could help you. Estimate the work it would take to roll out such automations and have an open dialog with your team and managers to explore the possibilities. Once you collectively agree on an automation to deploy, start the deployment and record the metrics to show progress. If you can show with metrics that your solution has reduced manual labor and saved multiple teams time, then you have data you can leverage to convince your company to take a more comprehensive program-level approach to DevSecOps.

We'll close with a few final tips gained from our experience in running DevSecOps programs:

*Identify the pain points that matter.*
> Everyone has something they want to fix, but focus on the things that matter most. Identify which issues affect productivity across the board and rank them by the magnitude of their impact, frequency of occurrence, or both.

*Start small, iterate often.*
> In your search for the perfect solution, don't get caught in "analysis paralysis," where you're using people's time (and thus money), but not generating anything useful. Don't shy away from building proofs of concept to demonstrate your ideas. Even if the proof of concept disproves your hypothesis, it still yields valuable data. Once you build your v1, ask the users which big-ticket items they want to see fixed. Prioritize them as you build your v2.

*Measure as much as you can.*
> When identifying a problem to solve, you need to ensure that the problem is worth solving. Data is important here too. If you can show that the problem occurs nearly every week and takes X number of hours for Y engineers to solve, you demonstrate a clear need to solve it. And once you have implemented a solution to address the problem, how do you show that it worked? Measurement. Using the same metrics you used to show the impact of the problem, you can demonstrate how the problem has declined after the solution was implemented, proving your solution's efficacy.

Building a successful DevSecOps program takes iteration and measurement. Everything else follows from that. If you have a team with the right mindset and skills, you can evolve to solve bigger problems at your workplace.

# Summary

As you finish this book, we hope you have learned to recognize the right people, the right tools, and the right approach to begin your DevSecOps journey. It is important to find the right partners for this journey, so make sure your team is also excited and determined to move in the right direction.

A quick recap of key takeaways from this chapter:

- The size and composition of the roles on a team depend on your budget, and the company's needs. One size does not fit all.

- Your DevSecOps program/initiative should include a team of developers, security engineers, and a product manager. This team's primary function is to build and maintain applications that support the principles of DevSecOps.

- At its inception, your DevSecOps program/initiative should include a compliance team; this should not be a last-minute addition.
- Ensure consistent communication within your team and with your stakeholders, ideally by way of a concise status report. Transparent communication breeds trust and encourages data-driven reasoning.
- Developers who build misconfigurations into their applications should be accountable for remediating them. The security team can assist them, but the originators of the misconfigurations should be the driving force of remediation.
- Use threat models and document architectural patterns as you see them. Having a library of modular patterns promotes the creation of reusable, secure architectures.
- Give your security team time to prevent recurring misconfigurations. Security teams should not be fighting fires every day. If there is a recurring problem, allow your security team to spend time investigating the root cause and fixing it.

# Index

detection of system vulnerabilities, 36, 40, 44, 69-70, 75, 81, 85

detective security controls, 24, 62-63

developers, DevSecOps, 6, 8, 23, 24-26, 63, 88-89, 93

DevOps, 4-7, 10

DevSecOps, 6

    (see also SaC (Security as Code))

    about, 6-7

    as adaptive toolchain, 68, 84, 88

    Chaos experiment in CI/CD pipeline in, 76

    collaborative operations of, 4, 90-91

    culture of, 4, 10, 68

    first steps and priorities with, 95

    People-Process-Technology triad in, 5, 10, 59, 87-96

    with security built-in early in life cycle, 1, 25, 26-34, 62, 68-70, 90

    security checks in, 6-7, 9

disruptive simulations, 76

Distributed Denial of Service (DDoS) attacks, 39

distributed systems, 67-68, 71

Docker Engine, 14, 15

downtime, costs of and minimizing, 69-70

doxware, 37

DPI (deep packet inspection) testing, 69

## E

EBS volumes, FIS experiment on, 84

EC2 instances (see Amazon EC2 instances)

Effective DevOps (Davis and Daniels), 4

egress and ingress traffic, 53-55, 83

EKS (Elastic Kubernetes Service), 13, 17-19, 79

EKS Cluster product, 17, 19

EKS Lambda product, 18, 19

EKS logging product, 18

EKS Nodegroup, 18

EKS Virtual Private Cloud (VPC), 18, 49, 53-55

elevation of privilege security risk, 24

EMF (CloudWatch Embedded Metric Format), 41

encryption/encryption-at-rest, 2, 8, 43

endpoints, cyber attacks on, 38

engineer teams (see security engineers)

Equifax data breach, 38

escalation of access privileges, 37

evaluation of problems, holistic tools for, 59, 74, 90

event, defined, 51

EventBridge events, 78

    with alerts on CloudWatch alarms, 53

    with AWS Config evaluation, 50

    with CodeCommit repository changes, 29

experiments (see Chaos Engineering)

## F

fail and error messages, 31-33, 66, 82

failure testing, 31-33, 70

Fault Injection Simulator (FIS), 76-85

fault injection testing, 70, 71, 76-85

filtering of data in logs, 36, 44, 45, 51

fintech, 44

FIS (Fault Injection Simulator), 76-85

Flow Logs, VPC, 53-55

Fowler, Martin, 67

## G

Gandhi, Raju, 22

GetMetricData, 46

git commit command, 65

Git repository, 14, 16, 22, 28

GitHub repository, 23, 26, 76

goals for security teams, 90, 92, 95

Graz University of Technology, 81

GuardDuty, 62, 63

## H

hard real-time distributed systems, 68

Hashicorp Terraform, 6, 21, 89

Head First Git (Gandhi), 22, 28

How to Measure Anything (Hubbard), 92

How to Measure Anything in Cybersecurity Risk (Hubbard), 92

Hubbard, Douglas W., 92

human identities, 57, 61

hypotheses in Chaos experiments, 72, 74

## I

IaC (Infrastructure as Code)

    defined, 2

    languages for, 6, 21, 89

    pipeline for, 17-19

    software installation for, 13-16

    standardized templates in, 8

IaC, security for, 21-34, 87-96

    about, 2, 21, 33

example of, 23, 27-34
IAM checkers for prevention of, 29-31, 33
recommending fixes for, 10
team accountability for, 93, 97
MitM (man-in-the-middle) attack, 37
monitoring
    versus logging, 35
    of network with VPC, 53-55
monolithic architectures, 67
Morris, Kief, 2, 5
mTLS (mutual Transport Layer Security), 94

N

naming of resources, standardized, 60
Netflix, 71
network ACL (network access control list), 53, 54
network monitoring with VPC, 53-55
network surveillance testing, 69
NIST 800-53 standards, 58

O

observability, 36
open source tooling, shell scripting for, 89
OpenTelemetry, 41
operating system vulnerabilities, 81
operations in software development, 1, 3-7
outages, costs of and minimizing, 69-70

P

PaaS (platform as a service), 14
Parliament open source tool, 65-66
passive cyber attacks, 38
pattern matching for anomaly detection, 45, 46
patterns, reusable modular, 94, 97
pay-as-you-consume approach, 69
people in DevSecOps, 59, 87-93
People-Process-Technology framework, 5, 10, 59, 87-96
permission policy example, 61
permissions boundaries, 63
permissions in IAM, assigning, 22, 58-60, 66
pipelines
    about, 25
    building basic, 17-19
    for Chaos experiments, 75-78
    CI/CD, 76
    with CodePipeline, 28-33

committing code for, 25-31
IAM, 60, 63-66
logs of, 31-33
for preventing security misconfigurations, 27-34
security in software development of, 6
platform as a service (PaaS), 14
pod stress test, Kubernetes, 79
port 22 access, example with, 25, 27
"Predictability: Does the Flap of a Butterfly's Wings in Brazil Set Off a Tornado in Texas?" (Lorenz), 70
predictive security controls, 68
preventive security controls, 25-33, 36, 62, 68-70, 75
principle of least privilege, 58-60, 66
Principles of Chaos Engineering manifesto, 71-76
privileges, elevation and escalation of access, 24, 37, 58-60, 66
process in DevSecOps, 5, 10, 59, 92-95, 96
    (see also teams, DevSecOps)
procurement of tools, 10
product managers, 90, 95
production environments
    Chaos experiments in, 75
    IAM controls and, 61
    reducing risk to, 76
Python
    about, 14, 89
    AWS SDK for, 8
    checking version of, 15

R

RaaS (Ransomware as a service), 37, 38
RACI charts (responsibility assignment matrices), 11, 93
random actions, effects of, 71
ransom payments, 38
ransomware attacks, 36-38
RCA (root cause analysis), 40, 46, 51-53, 70
real-time distributed systems, 67
real-world events, simulation of, 74
relationships, direct and indirect, 48
remediation, AWS Config rules for, 48-51
reporting, 89, 92
    (see also compliance reporting)
repositories (see CodeCommit repository)
repudiation security risk, 24

## About the Authors

**BK Sarthak Das** is a security engineer at Google. He was previously a senior security architect at AWS and has helped multiple Fortune 500 customers in securing their cloud environments. BK started his career as a full-stack web developer and grew into the security domain, which led him to get his master's from the University of Washington (Seattle) with a focus on cybersecurity. BK has published multiple AWS tech blogs and regularly builds solutions that can be adopted by AWS users.

**Virginia Chu** is a principal DevSecOps engineer at AWS. She works with enterprise-scale customers around the globe to design and implement a variety of solutions in the cloud. Virginia started as a Linux system administrator and developer, wearing many hats. She's self-taught, so in her spare time she's digging deep and trying to learn everything she doesn't already know. Virginia has published AWS tech blogs and provides modern solutions to the cloud community.

## Colophon

The animal on the cover of *Security as Code* is a San Diego horned lizard (*Phrynosoma blainvillii*), also known as a horny toad. They predominantly live on the southern Pacific coast of California in habitats with sandy soils that are low in vegetation. They are diurnal and are active in warm weather but inactive during periods of cold or extreme heat, when they will bury themselves in loose soil. They primarily eat ants, as well as other small invertebrates.

The horns on their heads and the pointed scales on their upper body and tail give them their name. These lizards tend to be small, ranging from 2.5 to 4.5 inches in snout length, with females being slightly larger than males. Their bodies are flat, oval-shaped, and predominantly red, brown, yellow, or gray with dark spots. The smooth scales of their bellies range from cream and beige to yellow with dark spots. The color of their bodies can also adapt slightly to their surroundings.

When evading predators, San Diego horned lizards take advantage of camouflage and remain motionless. When threatened, their bodies inflate with air, making them difficult to swallow. They also make warning noises, bite, and stab with their horns. As a last resort, they can spit blood from the corners of their eyes.

Their current IUCN conservation status is of Least Concern. Many of the animals on O'Reilly covers are endangered; all of them are important to the world.

The cover illustration is by Karen Montgomery, based on an antique line engraving from *Animal Life In the Sea and On the Land*. The cover fonts are Gilroy Semibold and Guardian Sans. The text font is Adobe Minion Pro; the heading font is Adobe Myriad Condensed; and the code font is Dalton Maag's Ubuntu Mono.

# O'REILLY®

# Learn from experts.
# Become one yourself.

Books | Live online courses
Instant Answers | Virtual events
Videos | Interactive learning

# Get started at oreilly.com.

CPSIA information can be obtained
at www.ICGtesting.com
Printed in the USA
JSHW042237050123
35833JS00004B/21